MIND IT

TO

FIND IT

A path towards inner success

JOT SINGH

AKNOWLEDGEMENTS

Dedicated to my parents, who always taught me the lessons of honesty and simplicity. I am grateful to my wife, Sarita for her continuous support for my writing. Special thanks to my daughter, Gitel; her contribution is indispensable in accomplishing this volume. Also, it won't be fair if I don't acknowledge Kanika, my niece and my son Yatharth for their contributions. I acknowledge the wealth of ideas, quotes, and examples drawn from diverse sources like books, videos, journals and study material that match my thinking process and have shaped this book. Special thanks to my corporate and spiritual trainers whose influence is reflected throughout. Credit for valuable insights goes to their wisdom; any shortcomings are solely my responsibility. My prime goal is to assist reader to the best of my abilities. while I have made an effort to credit the original thought wherever I have quoted them, I still offer my sincere apologies for any inadvertent inclusions made unknowingly.

CONTENTS

PREFACE

Buckle up for a heartfelt journey with "Mind It to Find It." Beyond words, this book serves as a simple yet powerful guide to reshape your thinking, cultivate a positive inner-self, and find internal success. A gentle reminder: it's not for the faint hearted but for those seeking change, wisdom, and a calm mind.

Unraveling life's complexities, the book provides very simple and practical tools for graceful navigation through challenges. It encourages reflection, prompting small but meaningful changes in your outlook. Invest time in these interconnected chapters for not just personal growth but also a positive impact on your life and of those around you.

In the simplicity of its message, "Mind It to Find It" becomes a companion on your journey of self-discovery and transformation. Emphasizing responsiveness, keen observations, and the beauty of nature as life disciplines, connect with nature and tap into its natural intelligence. Regardless of age or gender, this book offers valuable insight for all who seek positive transformation.

INTRODUCTION

We all want to succeed in life, but there are several aspects to it. Achieving success requires physical fitness, as a healthy body supports a healthy mind. When your body is in good shape, you're better equipped to pursue your goals, and a well-maintained mind thrives in a healthy body.

Then comes your mental health, which begins with understanding the brain. The brain, being a physical organ, receives instructions from the mind. Therefore, understanding the dynamics of both the conscious and subconscious mind is crucial. Developing this awareness marks the beginning of a journey into one's inner world.

This journey often sparks a quest for inner peace and happiness. The key to finding these qualities often lies in aligning oneself with nature. Observing this alignment leads to true intelligence. Realizing this true intelligence fosters a stable personality that earns respect in society. With a stable inner foundation, you transcend psychological illusions and engage with the real world with gratitude, continually striving to contribute positively to society.

PHYSICAL HEALTH

Nurturing fitness

"He who has health has hope, and he who has hope has everything."

– Thomas Carlyle.

The sun was blazing hot, and the King and his soldiers embarked on a hunting expedition. They chased the prey deep into the forest, but suddenly, the King realized he was lost. With no idea where to go, no food or water left, the King began to feel desperate. But just when he thought all hope was lost, he heard a rustling in the bushes.

To his great relief, it was a woodcutter, he discovered a woodcutter who was going about his daily work. The woodcutter promptly recognized the King's royal attire and bowed to him respectfully. The King, parched and hungry, begged for water and food, which the kind-hearted woodcutter gladly offered.

Once the King had quenched his thirst and appeased his hunger, the woodcutter guided him back to the palace. The King was so impressed by the woodcutter's generosity and kindness that he invited him to the palace as an esteemed guest. The ecstatic woodcutter returned home and narrated the entire incident to his wife, who was overjoyed to hear about her husband's unexpected stroke of luck.

The very next day, the woodcutter found himself standing in the palace's main hall, surrounded by soldiers, who were shocked by his unexpected presence.

The King, who was impressed by the woodcutter's selflessness, realized that he had to do something to help end the woodcutter's poverty. Recalling his Sandalwood Garden an idea sprouted in king's mind. He prompted, "Who better than a woodcutter to take care of my prized possession?"

With that in mind, the King gifted the sandalwood garden to the woodcutter, who was over the moon with excitement. The woodcutter knew that this gift would change his fortunes for the better. But little did he know, he was in for a big surprise.

As it turned out, the woodcutter had spent his entire life cutting trees and burning them into coal to make a living. He did the same with the sandalwood trees, thinking they were just other wood. Time passed, and one day the King decided to visit the garden and see how it was being maintained.

To his shock and horror, the entire garden was destroyed. The once thriving garden was now in ruins with only a few trees remaining at a place or two. The King was mortified, but he didn't lose his cool. Instead, he asked the woodcutter what had happened. The woodcutter replied, "My lord, you are so kind. I am so thankful to you for the garden. Because of your gift, I can now sell so much coal. It has improved my living conditions."

The King realized that he had made a grave mistake by gifting the sandalwood garden to the woodcutter, who had no idea of its true worth. In an attempt to rectify the situation. The king gave the him a small piece of sandalwood and asked him to sell it in the market.

To his astonishment the woodcutter discovered that the value of the small piece of sandalwood was many times greater than that of coal. Overwhelmed by this revelation he came back, fell on the King's feet, and humbly asked for forgiveness for the blunder he had made by burning down the trees due to his lack of knowledge.

Stupid woodcutter, isn't he? But in real life, we are the woodcutters, with the sandalwood garden being our body and the King, the creator of the Universe.

The story of the woodcutter reminds us that we are all like him in some ways. We are given a precious gift by the universe: Our body. This is the most beautiful, efficient, sophisticated machine ever created. We must take care of it as if it were a priceless garden, with constant maintenance and care. The question is, are we doing it justice?

The human body is a work of art, an intricate and beautiful masterpiece created by the universe. It is a machine that operates with flawless precision, performing miraculous processes every minute that we take for granted. It's as if we were given a Lamborghini, but instead of treating it with care and maintenance, we take it off-roading every day and forget to change the oil.

Indeed, our bodies are the key to unlocking greatness in all areas of our lives, whether it be social, economic, or spiritual. However, amidst the chaos and demands of our fast-paced lives, we often overlook the very element that makes everything else possible. We push ourselves to the limit, sometimes neglecting our health for productivity and convenience. The reality is, without a healthy body, we cannot hope to achieve anything truly great. It's like trying to drive a car with a flat tire. It's not going to get you very far, and it might even cause a permanent damage.

Our bodies are not indestructible, but they do have a built-in alarm system. They give us warning signs when things are amiss, like a flickering check engine light. Yet all too often, we ignore these signs until it's too late.

It's time to start treating our bodies like the precious works of art that they truly are. We must learn to nourish them, care for them, and attentively heed their needs. As the wise Bella Bleue once said, "Your body has great wisdom. Trust in it. Learn from it. Nourish it. Watch your life transform and be healthy."

Let's no longer take this incredible gift for granted. It's time to treat our bodies with the respect and care they deserve, and by doing so, we can unlock the full potential of our lives. And embark on a journey with our Lamborghini of a body and enjoying every moment of the ride.

Health and Wellness:

Think about it – Fancy cars, lavish comforts, and all that glitz can lose their charm when our health takes a hit. Without a strong body and clear mind life's adventure can feel like a bumpy ride. So how can we keep the zest alive in all stages of life? Is it doable?

Health is not just the absence of disease.

It's a state of body and mind that allows us to perform all necessary activities in life.

Advances in science and technology have increased life expectancy, yet it's robust health that adds life to these years. Live healthy you will not just add years to your journey- you'll add life. At 25, we'll be as energetic as our 18-year-old self and when we are in our fifties we'll feel as vibrant as if we were 30

Time to unveil a health secret that's cooler than a spy thriller Here is the deal: Our bodies like a good balance –not too much not too little, just the Goldilocks spot. We can think of it as harmony between action and relaxation. Pushing too Hard work without rest is like running marathon in high heels – not the smoothest journey. And lounging all the day? Well, our bodies are more adventurous than couch potatoes. Now let's change things up when it comes to being healthy. Doctors and medicines do their part no doubt, but do you know the real heroes are? Exercise and eating wisely. Think about it: this dynamic pair can take on 80% of health problems like champions.

It's often believed that spending on wellness is expensive, but the truth is dealing with illness costs way more.

Many diseases originate from an unhealthy lifestyle, where we disregard healthy food and good habits until illness strikes. We then consult doctors and take pills, often unaware that every pill has its side effects. It's time to break free from this loop and proactively embrace wellness to lead a healthy and happy life.

Here is an interesting fact: Our immune system serves as our inner doctor, and the stronger it is, the better our overall health becomes. A resilient immune system battles various illnesses, facilitates healing and maintains our well- being. A solid immunity means that we rely less on external medicines for recovery. The COVID pandemic has reminded us of the importance of immunity, highlighting how individuals with strong immunity fare better against the Virus.

In nut shell its essential to prioritize physical work and nutrition, fortify our immune system, cultivate awareness of wellness. With these habits, we can enhance the quality of years and lead a life that's both healthy and joyful

Embrace the Glory of Mornings

Are you ready to kick start your day with a bang? Heeding Robin Sharma's wisdom "Take excellent care of the front end of your day, and the rest of the day will pretty much take care of itself. Own your morning, elevate your life, "certainly, it's like stepping onto a path of truth. And what better moment to elevate your life than in the tranquil embrace of early morning?"

Let's admit it, the world can be a bit messy. However, the early morning hours are a rare exception, untouched by both external and internal pollution. While most of us are still cozily tugged in bed, the threat of environmental pollution is at its lowest. And with fewer distractions, we are less likely to entertain unnecessary or even sinful thoughts, thus reducing the risk of internal pollution.

If you're not yet persuaded, then let the wisdom of our ancient Vedic system work its magic on you. The system emphasizes the importance of waking up early and tuning your life to align with your goals. In fact, this practice has been adopted by global billionaires and influential leaders across the globe.

In line with the Vedic philosophy, awaking 1.5 hours before dawn during the Brahma Muhurta is the key to unlocking the full potential of your day. During this time, the air's oxygen is at its best. Breathing in this fresh oxygen can help reducing stress, boost your energy levels, and even improve your immunity.

But here is the question: what is the Brahma Muhurta?

It is the time that starts 2 Muhurtas (equal to 48 minutes each) before sunrise and ends 48 minutes before sunrise. This magical window of time. However, this enchanting timeframe can vary based on geographical location and the changing time of sunrise across different seasons.

So, why not try waking up early and relishing the morning glory? You might discover that it's the perfect way to start your day with a fresh outlook and a revived sense of purpose.

Benefits of waking up in Brahma Muhurta

Wow, what a fascinating piece of research on the benefits of morning exercise! As per the International Journal of Yoga and Allied Sciences, the pre-dawn period is a time when nascent oxygen is available in the atmosphere, which can easily mix with hemoglobin to form oxyhemoglobin. This process provides a host of benefits, such as boosting energy, strengthening immunity, maintaining the balance of blood pH, reducing pain, soreness, and cramps, and enhancing the absorption of minerals and vitamins.

But beyond the science, there's something magical about the morning hours. Have you ever felt the crispness of the air at dawn? It's truly a beautiful gift that we can experience every day.

Picture this: You wake up before sunrise, have refreshing glass of water, freshen up and get ready to embrace the day with the universe. Mornings are the perfect time to plan and set intentions, as our minds and bodies are naturally calm and centered.

To gain and retain energy throughout the day, physical exercise is crucial. Whether it's walk, jog, run, bike ride, swim, yoga and pranayama or playing sports, engaging in physical activity for 40 to 60 minutes each morning in fresh air is essential for overall wellness. Exercise is indeed our medicine, so let's lace up those morning shoes and make it a habit.

But let's face it, forming new habits can be a real uphill battle especially when the cozy bed is calling your name and snooze button is your best friend. However, the transformation n that comes with making exercise a non –negotiable is worth every bit of the effort. Think about it –regular exercise is not all about looking and feeling fabulous it's your secret weapon for shedding those extra pounds, gaining muscle, and boosting your overall fitness game.so it's time to say "goodbye" to snooze button and "hello" to your new fitness adventure

As Kenneth H. Cooper wisely put it, "The reason I exercise is for the quality of life I enjoy." When you exercise regularly your body releases hormones like serotonin, endorphins, and BDNF (Brain-Derived Neurotropic Factor), all of which are your mood's best friend. These hormones team up to make you feel happier, less stressed and super motivated.

And as we get older, three things become increasingly important for our health: brain function, exercise, and our mood. In a 2004 European study, they focused at how these three factors are connected. And what they found was pretty cool. They discovered that the better your brain works as you age, the more likely you are to keep moving. And guess what? The more you move the happier you tend to be with fewer bouts of feeling down.

Recent research hints that there is a twist in the exercise brain-health story. It seems that the relationship between the two might be more interesting than we thought. your brain health can influence how well and our exercise habits can, in turn, impact our brain. It's like a dance between the two.

So, let's embrace the magic of the morning hours and turn exercise a daily ritual. It's moment to put our physical and mental well- being front and center and the rewards are boundless

The magic of mornings beckons – let's seize it

The TEMPA Theory

Have you ever found yourself searching for shortcuts or ways to do things with minimal effort? Well, according to "TEMPA Theory", you're not alone! This theory of Effort Minimization in Physical Activity suggests that as humans, we tend to opt for the path of least resistance. However, this approach may not be beneficial in the long run. The TEMPA theory further explains that as we engage in less physical activity, our brain capacity decreases, and we become programmed to minimize our physical activity as we age.

But, here's the good news - we can overcome this by preserving our brain function and remaining active!

Studies show that older adults who engage in physical activities experience less depression, making it crucial for people in their 40s, 50s, and 60s to focus on self-care. To achieve this, one must focus on SELF: Sleep, Exercise, Love, and Food.

So, if you want to keep yourself mentally and physically fit, make sure to prioritize SELF-CARE. Get enough sleep, engage in regular exercise, prioritize love and relationships, and nourish your body with healthy food. By doing so, you can overcome the TEMPA theory and enjoy a happy, healthy life!

Food and nutrition

Food is not just something we consume to satisfy our hunger; it's also our medicine. What, when, and how we eat play a major role in defining our overall health. Imagine your diet as symphony perfectly balanced and loaded with nutritious. It's your source of boundless energy, yet it also leaves you light and refreshed.

In the heart of Taif, Kingdom of Saudi Arabia a study embarked on a critical mission back in 2007. Its quest? To investigate the effects of food habits and lifestyle on the prevalence of overweight/obesity among schoolchildren in the area.

Saudi Arabia is a country with a large youth population and had witnessed a profound shift in the way of life in recent years. As modernity embraced the nation so did significant changes in how people lived and ate. But there was a big problem: lots of young people were becoming overweight and obese. It was like a dark cloud hanging over them.

When children carry excess weight, they have a tendency to remain so into adulthood, which can lead to a host of health problems, including heart disorders, hypertension, lessening cerebral blood flow, asymptomatic coronary heart atherosclerosis, high risk of type 2 diabetes mellitus, hypogonadism, and more.

Being overweight or obese doesn't just affect your body; it also has social and economic effects. These include low self-esteem, poor body image, and having trouble in moving and working.

In the Taif area, they discovered that around 27.5% of kids had a weight problem. Boys had it bit more than girls (31.9% versus 21.9%) and it was also more common among school children from high-income families.

The reason behind that was not a mystery. Bad eating habits, played a big roll like skipping breakfast, low consumption of fruits and vegetables, low milk uptake, and increased consumption of soft drinks and high-calorie drinks- that's where the problem lurked.

Research has shown that the kids who carry extra weight tend to move less and watch more TV than their slimmer peers, not just in Saudi Arabia but in 34 countries around the world, in the category of age 10 - 16 years.

This lack of physical activity is a key player in the overweight and obesity game. and it can mess with your blood fat levels. For example, research found that inactive Saudi boys have unfavorable blood lipid profiles compared to active boys.

Maintaining good health, it's all about being mindful of our food habits and patterns. Remember that 30% of food is digested in the mouth, which is why it's important to take time to chew food properly until it gets homogeneously mixed with your saliva. Raw foods are like treasure chest of nutrients such as protein, fiber, micronutrients, and carbohydrates, which our body absorbs the most.

Therefore, our healthy eating plate should have a bit of everything: veggies, fruits, whole grains, healthy protein, healthy oils, and water. When we cook food, some of the nutrients get lost, so aiming for at least 50% raw food in our diet is a smart move. Raw leafy greens are easily to digest and keep our energy levels up

And don't forget the daily dose of seasonal fruits and nuts: they are like nature's medicine. Eat your fruits before food, not with or after food, as they get digested very fast.

By making conscious choices about what, how and when we eat, we can take responsibility for our health and ensure that the food we consume nourishes each cell in our body. Just as a car needs quality fuel, our bodies require nutritious food to function efficiently. So, let's feed ourselves in such a way that fuels our health and not just our bellies.

Building a Healthy and Balanced Diet

The Harvard School of Public Health has put forward a useful guideline for creating a healthy plate.

According to the Harvard school of public health, a healthy plate consists of the following:

Vegetables and fruits – ½ of your plate.

Aim for color and variety, and remember that potatoes don't count as vegetables on the Healthy Eating Plate because of their negative impact on blood sugar.

Whole grains – ¼ of your plate.

Whole and intact grains—whole wheat, barley, wheat berries, quinoa, oats, brown rice. They have a milder effect on blood sugar and insulin than white bread, white rice, and other refined grains.

Protein power – ¼ of your plate.

Fish, poultry, beans, and nuts are all healthy, versatile protein sources. They can be mixed into salads and pair well with vegetables on a plate. Limit red meat, and avoid processed meats such as bacon and sausage.

Healthy plant oils – in moderation.

Choose healthy vegetable oils like olive, canola, soy, corn, sunflower, peanut, and others, and avoid partially hydrogenated oils containing unhealthy trans fats. Remember that "low-fat" does not mean "healthy."

By following these guidelines, you can create a healthy plate that promotes good nutrition and overall health.

It's like a simple recipe for healthier you!

Water, the Elixir of Life

Water is just not a drink; its secret source of life itself. It's not just a thirst quencher, but plays a crucial role in maintaining our body temperature, protecting our tissues, spinal cord, and joints. Think of it as bodies best friend, always there to keep things running smoothly. Let's look into the importance of water, the liquid life line that keeps us thriving:

A) Hydration

Water constitutes more than 60% of our body- it's our life blood. Drinking water helps in flushing out waste from our digestive system and supports our cardiovascular system. It also optimizes our brain function, allowing us to stay focused and alert. It's like backstage crew of a block buster movie. working tirelessly to keep everything in order

B) The danger of dehydration

Dehydration is a severe condition that can cause unclear thinking, mood changes, overheating, constipation, and even kidney stones. Picture this: Dehydration is like a villain snaking into your life, causing chaos. It messes with your thinking, makes you grumpy and even can lead to kidney stone! But worry not because staying hydrated is your super hero cape can prevent dehydration, leading to a happy and healthy life. Additionally, consuming water helps manage body weight and reduces calorie intake when substituted for sugary drinks.

C) The science of happiness

Numerous studies reveal a magical link between hydration and happiness. Well-hydrated people generally report being happier, more focused, and more alert. On the flip side, dehydrated individuals typically report being less content, confused, and unhappy. So, keep that water flowing for a daily dose of joy

D) Customized Hydration

The amount of water required by the body varies from person to person, and it's not a one-size-fits-all solution. Generally, 2-3 liters of water are sufficient under normal circumstances, but it depends on your body and lifestyle. Our hydration needs are unique to each of us. Exercise, hot weather, high altitude, high-fiber diet, caffeine/ alcohol indulgences all play a role.

It's essential to remember that our body receives water from food, but it is usually less than 20% of our total water intake. Therefore, relying only on solid foods for hydration is practically impossible. At the same time, consuming excessive water can also cause issues with our bodies, so we must understand our body's requirements and drink water accordingly.

E) Ageless Hydration

Older adults often don't sense thirst as much as younger adults and may be on medication that causes fluid loss. Therefore, it's crucial to keep track of our water intake, especially as we age.

F) Timming is everything

Start your day with a refreshing glass of water, since our body remains without water for 6-8 hours during sleep. But hold off on drinking water immediately after meals. It is not a healthy habit as it hinders digestion. The best time to drink water is before taking a meal or in the middle of a meal.

After waking up or exercising, it's essential to hydrate our body with a glass of water or more, depending on our body's requirements.

In conclusion, water is the life line, so we must drink enough water daily to keep our body healthy and happy. Let's make drinking water a habit and stay hydrated to live a healthy and fulfilling life.

Rejuvenate your body, enjoy sound sleep

Late-night sleeping has become a societal norm these days. We are like night owls, addicted to screens, chasing alerts and binge- watching shows until dawn. Many students prefer to stay up late to study and sending late-night birthday wishes have all become a part of our routine. But there is a price to pay for this life style: sleep deprivation. It's like a hidden cost we overlook.

It is high time we recognize that sound sleep is not a luxury; it's a necessity for our health. Sleep is also your body's rejuvenating elixir and a day without sound night sleep can leave you feeling utterly drained without doing any work.

Sleep is bodies superhero. It is in charge of fixing of muscle organizing your memory and managing the hormones which are responsible for growth and appetite. But when you skip sleep, it means you send your superhero on vacation. And the result? An increased risk of developing obesity and weight gain. It can also increase your appetite and make you more likely to eat foods high in sugar and fat. Plus, it's like a brain fog that affects your concentration, productivity, and performance.

So, make sure you give your body the required sleep.

A study published on 1st September 2015 revealed something eye-opening: that participants who slept fewer than 5 hours per night were 4.5 times more likely to develop a cold than those who enjoyed a sound sleep more than 7 hours.

But there is more to the story Sleep loss, especially from disturbed sleep, kicks off inflammation in your body. Which leads to a higher level of undesirable markers of inflammation like C-reactive protein and interleukin-6. Over time, this inflammation party can lead to chronic issues like obesity, heart disease, certain types of cancers, Alzheimer's disease, and depression.

If you're wondering about the magic number - how many hours are good for night's sleep? Well, it's not about the hours on clock; it's all about quality of your sleep. Some people can rejuvenate their bodies after a sound sleep of 3-4 hours, while others need 6 to 8 hours to recharge their batteries.

Mind your Posture

Ever found yourself stuck in a never-ending saga of bad posture? Maybe its hours of slouching over your desk or lounging on one leg like a casual flamingo. Whatever it is, it's time to put end to it and give your body the love it deserves.

Say good bye to discomfort of being stuck up in one position and don't worry, it's not as complicated as it sounds!

It's as simple as changing the things up!

First things first, take a break every hour or so to move around and stretch your muscles.

Take a lap around the office or do a quick yoga flow. Whatever gets your blood flowing and your body moving.

Next, adjust your posture throughout the day.

Try sitting up straight with your feet flat on the ground, or standing with your weight evenly distributed.

And don't forget to stretch! A few minutes of shoulder rolls, spinal twists, or hip openers can make all the difference.

But why stop there? Let's make it fun! Gather your coworkers and turn your posture switch-ups into a game. Try balancing on one foot or doing squats during your breaks. Or, challenge each other to a yoga pose-off.

Not only will you be taking care of your body, but you'll be bonding with your coworkers and having a blast while doing it.

Taking care of your body is crucial, and the posture switch-up is a simple yet effective way to do it. By switching up your posture regularly, taking stretch breaks, and getting creative, you'll prevent damage to your body and have fun doing it. So, let's get moving and give our bodies the love they deserve

What to avoid:

While occasional enjoyment of fast food is acceptable, it's important to avoid making it a regular part of your meals.

Now let's talk about drugs: don't even go there! Unfortunately, it's a hard reality that many young people are drawn to the experimenting with drugs because of easily accessibility in nearly every corner of the city. But let me warn you, even a single encounter with drugs can turn your life upside down.

Now, onto alcohol and smoking. It's important to remember that moderation is key when it comes to alcohol. Regular drinking can lead to severe health issues down the line, that's why it's better to limit your intake, or even better, consider quitting altogether. Your health will thank you.

When it comes to as for smoking, there's just no good reason to start. It's a health wrecker short cut to a shorter life. So, let's make smart choices, look out for our future and prioritize our health above all else!

Define fitness, measure fitness and award fitness

Cardiovascular endurance: Aerobic fitness, is the key to unlocking your body's full potential. It's about your body's ability to efficiently use oxygen and fuel your muscles and tissues through your heart, lungs and vessels. The best part? You can boost it with regular exercise! Weather it's running to cycling, swimming to brisk walking, you have got many ways to pump up your cardiovascular system and improve your endurance. This is all about power - the ability to produce force during a single maximal effort.

Whether you're lifting weights or doing resistance exercises you'll be building the kind of strength that allows you to lift heavy objects and perform physical tasks like a champ.

Muscular endurance: Think stamina - the ability to resist fatigue and maintain tension or repeated muscular contractions over time. This is where exercises like push-ups, planks, squats, and sit-ups come in - they'll give you the staying power to push through when the things get tough.

Flexibility And let's not forget about flexibility! The ability to move your joints through their full range of motion is crucial for maintaining good posture, preventing injuries, and feeling your best. Yoga is a superstar in the flexibility game. It's like a two for one deal - flexibility and stress reduction rolled into one.

Body composition Body composition is all about finding the right balance between fat and fat-free mass (muscle, bone, and water) in your body. By eating a healthy diet and incorporating strength training into your routine, you can maintain a healthy body composition and reduce your risk of chronic diseases like heart disease, diabetes, and cancer.

Now the big question: What are you waiting for? Dive into the world of fitness! Embrace the power of cardiovascular endurance and commit to a well-rounded fitness routine that includes strength training, flexibility, and healthy eating. Your body will thank you and you'll feel and look better, live a better life because of it!

DO IT YOURSELF

1. How would you personally interpret the concept of "health"?

2. When working towards a healthy lifestyle, what are the key factors you prioritize?

3. Are you familiar with the concept of the "inner doctor"? and if so, how does it assist you in maintaining your well-being?

4. Share your approach for selecting your food and meeting your nutritional needs.

5. Have you experienced any problems related to your posture? If so, what steps did you take to address them?

MENTAL SYNERGY

Brain and Mind

*"All limits exist only in the mind, and it is
only in the mind that they can be
overcome."*

— Alan Cohen

*"Our minds influence the key activity of
the brain, which then influences
everything; perception, cognition,
thoughts, feelings, and personal
relationships; they're all projections of
you."*

-Deepak Chopra.

If Life is like a catchy tune, good food and exercise make our bodies to dance in a healthy rhythm. Our thoughts and choices are the DJ that plays the beats of our mental well- being. By feeding our minds with good thoughts and conscious choices, we can achieve positive outcomes and optimal mental health.

When we refer to our mind, we are speaking of the collective mental processes that enable us to think, reason, and experience emotions. Our mind is responsible for our consciousness, thoughts, memories, and perceptions. It is the intangible essence of our being that defines who we are as individuals.

The brain, on the other hand, is the physical organ that serves as the control center for the nervous system. It receives and processes information from our senses, sends signals to our muscles and organs, and regulates our bodily functions. Brain science and cognitive psychology are two rapidly evolving fields that seek to understand how the brain works, and how we can optimize its performance. The brain operates like a sophisticated computer, constantly processing information and generating output in response to our sensory input. While other animals also possess a brain, humans have the unique ability to think and experience emotions with intelligence. By taking a holistic approach to health, and nurturing our body, mind, spirit and energy, we can achieve optimal health and well-being at any stage of life.

The human brain has three main parts:

1. Brain stem: - This is the bottom, stalk-like portion of your brain. It connects your brain to the spinal cord and it sends messages to the rest of your body to regulate breathing, heart rate, etc.

2. Cerebellum: This structure is located at the back of the brain, underlying the occipital and temporal lobes of the cerebral cortex. Despite comprising 10% of the brain volume, it contains 50% of the total number of neurons in the brain

3. Cerebrum: The cerebrum is the largest part of the brain, composed of the right and left hemispheres. One-half of the cerebrum controls muscle functions, speech, reading, writing, and learning of thoughts and emotions. The right hemisphere controls the muscles on the left part of the body and the left hemisphere

controls the muscles on the right position. Neuroscientists prove that the two sides of the brain collaborate to perform a wide variety of tasks.

The Neural network is what we need to know to understand brain functions. Neurons are the building blocks of brain functions and are essential for every action our brain carries out. Around 86 billion neurons are present in the brain and each neuron is connected to another 1000 neurons creating a complex communication network. Neurons are present both in our brains and our spinal cords.

Let us also dive into the fundamental aspects of brain signaling in a simple yet captivating way. Firstly, given below is the basic diagram of the neuron:

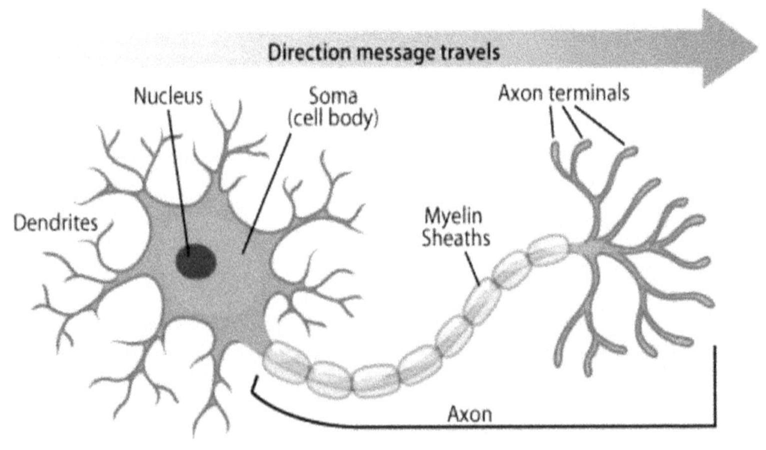

Let us understand brains working in following five points

1) When something happens (a stimulus) like touching a hot plate, it acts on the receptor, a chemical reaction begins in our body. This reaction produces an electric impulse.

2) This electric impulse is received by Dendrite like an eager messenger which sends it to AXON through the cell body

3) The axon is like long high way and at the end of the Axon, the electric impulse releases a tiny amount of chemical substance in the synapse.

4) This chemical substance crosses the gap (between the axons of two neurons) and starts a similar electrical pulse on the dendrite of the next neuron.

5) This process continues till the electrical impulse reaches the relay neuron in the brain through the spinal cord.

Our Nerves carry messages from sensory organs and muscles to the central nervous system and back. They also transmit and process signals within the central nervous system.

This is how the brain knows when something happens. The process consists of chemical signal -

electrical signals to chemical signals through neurons and the nervous system.

Through this complicated process, the brain controls the body based on signals. And our body follows brain signals.

Neuroscientists could find this process of the brain a few decades back and still, a lot of research is going on this most evolved organ in human beings. It is considered the most complicated and maximum energy-consuming organ of the body for its vital functions.

It governs the whole body. But can we understand the being of humans just by understanding the brain? Is our brain the 'mind' that drives us?

Modern science provides us with a detailed understanding of the brain, but the concept of mind is explained more thoroughly in the Vedic world. In spiritual and Vedic traditions, the brain is considered a part of the body like any other organ, with specific functions and limited memory. Instead, they focus on the mind, which is referred to as our consciousness. According to them our memory isn't in the brain; it is in every cell of our body and that the mind has a vast connection with the body and the universe. It is an interesting way to look at ourselves.

In contrast to the brain, the mind is composed of subtle matter of various grades of density with different rates of vibration. The mind has an energy field or aura or call it a psychic halo that emanates from it, which can be highly effulgent in developed minds. This aura can travel long way and positively affect many people under its influence.

In yoga, the brain is considered a space in the physical body that controls logical operations, but it is not regarded as synonymous with the mind. The mind encompasses all of our conscious and unconscious activities, including memories, beliefs, thoughts, feelings, and ego.

In Vedic philosophy, the mind is seen as composed of four parts or has a fourfold nature, which is also known as "Antahkarana Chatushtaya". These are:

A. Buddhi (The intellect)

B. Ahamkara (Identification/doership)

C. Manas (conscious mind)

D. Chitta (unconscious mind)

Each of these four parts of the mind has its unique function and plays a vital role in shaping our consciousness and overall mental wellness. When we understand these different aspects of the mind and nurture them, we can achieve a higher level of consciousness and live a more fulfilling life.

A) Buddhhi (Intellect)

Buddhi, or the intellect, is an essential part of the mind and plays a crucial role in decision-making. It is an instrument of survival based on the limited data we acquire from sensory perceptions, both conscious and unconscious. However, intellect alone is useless without any data, much like a phone without any information.

Just like different telephones have their own memories and data processing capabilities, humans also have various capacities of intellect.

The intellect can use different permutations and combinations of data to make decisions.

Ideally, the Buddhi should be the decision-making faculty of the mind. However, for it to be effective, it needs to function without being influenced by other aspects of the mind like Manas, Chitta, and Ahamkara. In other words, it needs to be free from biases, emotions, and other mental processes that can influence its decision-making abilities.

Therefore, it is important to cultivate and strengthen our Buddhi through conscious awareness, critical thinking, and rational analysis. By doing so, we can improve our decision-making abilities and make informed choices that benefit our overall well-being.

B) Ahamkara (Identification/doer ship):

Now let us dive into Ahamkara. This aspect of the mind deals with identity, the way you identify yourself. Ahamkara gives identity to the person and makes him or her unique. Ahamkara gives you sense of belongingness. For example, you think you belong to this country or this religion, cast, creed, gender, etc. According to this, your intellect will work. Here is the twist: Your intellect will constantly perform to protect that identity. It means intellect is the slave of the identity you have taken. It becomes the loyal servant of your chosen identity.

In the yogic system, Ahamkara takes central stage It's like the lead actor of drama of your life. The intellect will work accordingly to protect how you identify yourself. So, if your identity says this is right or wrong your intellect follows the suit. It's like personal bodyguard for who you are.

Although Ahmkara is a distinct and unique characteristic of the individual, there is the catch: This identity game, often leads to feelings of alienation, pain, or loneliness.

Feeling like you belong to a specific community, nation, or whatever essential for society's well-being. It's like being a part of team in the big game of life. But here is the thing: when you identify strongly with a group it can sometime feel like you are stuck in a box. You will be limited to this identity and cannot think beyond this because you function only from your intellect.

Because the intellect acts only along the axis of Ahamkara. (Ahamkara being the lead actor of drama and intellect being the bodyguard of ahamkara). In other words, the intellect takes its sustenance from Ahamkara. So, it cannot easily break free from this cycle.

But here is the exciting part: There are different ways and means to observe life beyond these identities we have taken. There are ways to breakout of this box and see life from a wider perspective. It's like opening a window to a world beyond the role we play to survive.

C) Manas (Conscious mind)

Manas is often described as the conscious mind as it is responsible for processing the sensory inputs that we receive from the external world. It analyzes and interprets the data received from the sensory organs and decides which information is important to be passed on to the other parts of the mind. Here is the twist: Manas does not have the final decision-making authority and relies on the Buddhi for that. It's like a detective who reports to a higher-up which in this case is buddhi, your decision maker.

The manas is also like a playful monkey swinging through the trees of your mind. Like a curious monkey it's easily drawn to our desires, wishes, attractions, and aversions, which can lead to mental difficulty.

It can question and doubt the information it receives, which can sometimes be beneficial but can also lead to confusion and indecisiveness. Therefore, it is important to train the Manas to focus and not get swayed by external distractions.

D) Chitta(The cosmic Intelligence)

Chitta is the subconscious mind (Achetan) also known as cosmic intelligence. It is universal intelligence working in us which is free of boundaries. This intelligence is like cosmic force quietly working without limits and boundaries connecting you to the very essence of creation.

Much of your subconsciousness consists of submerged memories and experiences thrown into the background but recoverable. The Chitta is like a calm lake and our thoughts are like waves upon the lake's surface. The name and form are the normal ways these waves rise. No wave can rise without the name and form.

The mental process is not limited to consciousness alone. The field of the subconscious world is much greater than that of the conscious world.

Only 10% of mental activities come under consciousness. Ninety percent of mental activities take place in the subconscious mind. Messages, when ready, pop up like a flash from the subconscious mind to the surface of the conscious mind through the trapdoor in the subconscious mind.

To add on, Chitta is often described as the storehouse of all the impressions and experiences that we have accumulated throughout our lives, including those from past lives. These impressions, also known as sanskara, shape our personality and behavior. The quality of our sanskara affects the purity of our Chitta, which in turn influences our actions and experiences in life.

In yoga, one of the main goals is to purify the Chitta by reducing negative sanskara and cultivating positive ones. This is done through various practices such as meditation, self-reflection, and karma yoga, which involves selfless service and action without attachment to the outcome.

When the Chitta is pure and free from negative sanskara, the individual is said to experience a state of inner peace, clarity, and wisdom. This can lead to a deeper understanding of one's true nature and connection to the universe, which is often referred to as self-realization or enlightenment.

If you touch this dimension of your mind, which is the linking point to one's consciousness, you do not have to wish for anything, and you do not have to dream of anything – the best possible thing that can happen to you will anyway happen. It's like stepping into a world where your deepest desires manifest naturally.

Chitta is compiling all your sanskara. If your Chitta is pure, your Ahamkara will be sattvic. Once you have access to your Chitta, it is also a multi-pointed telescope. It makes you see things that no one else can see – in every direction. Chitta is the last point of the mind which connects to the basis of creation within you. It connects you with your consciousness.

Interaction within the fourfold mind

The Fourfold Mind: Understanding the Coordinated Process of Interaction

In Vedic language, the fourfold mind is known as 'Ahkarana Chatuste'. It comprises of four parts: Manas (conscious mind), Buddhi (intellect), Ahamkara (identity), and Chitta (subconscious mind). Together, they work in a coordinated process to influence our thoughts, decisions, and actions.

The Manas is the owner of our sensory organs and is responsible for processing information from our five senses.

It collects and stores sanskara, or impressions, based on our experiences. However, the Manas is often inconsistent and cannot make decisions. That's where Buddhi comes in. Buddhi decides what is right or wrong, good or bad based on the information provided by Manas. Through dhyana (meditation), we can develop our Buddhi and make better decisions.

Ahamkara is our identity or sense of doership. It influences our actions and decisions based on how we identify ourselves. There are three types of Ahamkaras - Satvik, rajsik, and tamsik. If one identifies with a tamsik Ahamkara, they lose the sense of good and bad. If Ahamkara is Satvik, Buddhi will make pure decisions. It's essential to change our Ahamkara to purity to make better decisions.

Chitta is a storehouse of cosmic memory that collects all information from Manas and Buddhi. Chitta is programmed and can only be purified through Ahamkara. Ahamkara regulates Chitta, and changing Ahamkara to purity is the key to uplifting Chitta. Once Chitta contains purity, it gives us universal knowledge and lifts our life.

Let's understand the fourfold mind with a simple example. You are walking down the bustling city streets and a striking poster catches your eye. It's a poster of an action-packed movie about a heroic soldier who fearlessly sacrifices everything to protect the border of his country. Your senses kick into gear and they are like little detectives soaking up every detail of the poster.

But that's not all. The real magic happens when this sensory information enters the stage of your mind called Manas. It's like whirlwind of data, swirling around seeking order and meaning. The correct matches are thrown into the Chitta along with the incoming data.

Now let us see what ahamkara does at this stage. Your Ahamkara identifies you as a true nationalist and patriotic person. This identity like a powerful guiding force starts to influence your Manas and Buddhi, the decision maker of the group. It's like your inner patriot whispers," You have to watch this movie. it's your duty!"

Buddhi steps up and confidently gives a green signal (decision) to watch this movie as it's strongly influenced by patriotism(ahamkara).I t is like an acknowledgement that cinematic experience perfectly aligns with your identity.

While enjoying the movie, something magical occurs: Certain scenes send shivers down your spine and goose bumps dance across your arms. These are not just movie moments they are like electric sparks that ignite your Chitta, leaving lasting impression in the form of samskaras.,

These samskaras become part of you, shaping your senility to national pride. And when in future right moment arrives these samskaras pop up like loyal allies, helping you to find perfect words and actions to express your patriotism.

Throughout your life cycle, you'll find yourself traversing realms of Manas, Buddhi, Chitta, and Ahamkara. Ahamkara is the regulator for Chitta, and we can purify Chitta only by changing our Ahamkara to purity.

By understanding the fourfold mind and developing our Buddhi, we can embark on a quest to make profound decisions that lead to a life filled with fulfillment and wisdom. Which will create an unshakable connection to your true self.

Yoga for mind

Yoga at its essence, represents the profound concept of union. It signifies the harmonious integration of mind, body and spirit. Through yogic practices, one can become aware of and regulate the layers of the mind.

Patanjali, an ancient Indian sage and scholar defines yoga in his seminal work, the "Yoga Sutras".

According to him the ultimate goal of Yoga is to attain a state of mental clarity, focus and tranquility. Maharishi Patanjali delineates the Eight limbs of yoga encompassing,

1) **Ethical Guidelines** (Yama and Niyama),

2) **Physical Postures** (Asanas) ,

3) **Breath Control** (Pranayama)

4) **Meditation** (Dhyana)

Practicing disciplines like Yamas and Niyamas help to cultivate a virtuous and disciplined mind. The art of pranayama or controlled breathing technique serves to bring the mind to a state of calmness and clarity. Meditation is a powerful tool enabling insight into the mind's workings, facilitating the release of negative impressions, and nurturing the cultivation of positive ones.

Through the regulation of mind via yogic practices, one can undo the wrong by cultivating positive impressions and behaviors. Instead of blaming the mind for wrongdoing, individuals can take responsibility for their actions and actively work towards correction. The goal of yoga is not to forget but to become more aware and mindful, to find union with oneself and the universe, and to live a life of purpose and meaning.

In conclusion, the mind is a powerful tool that influences our daily activities and experiences. Yoga offers a way to regulate the mind and cultivate positive impressions and behaviors. Through the practice of yoga, we can rectify missteps by addressing their roots and aligning ourselves with harmonious union with both self and the universe.

DO IT YOURSELF

1. Unpack the idea of the four-fold mind concept for better understanding.

2. How does Chitta play a significant role in our mental and emotional well-being?

3. Is Ahamkara synonymous with the concept of ego, or does it have a different meaning?

4. Which aspect of our mind is responsible for controlling our five senses?

5. In which part of our body is the mind located?

CONSCIOUS

&

SUBCONSCIOUS MIND

Harmony Unveiled

"The mind is its place and, in itself, can make a Heaven of Hell, a Hell of Heaven."

-John Milton

Building upon the previous chapter where we just explored the four facets of our mind as outlined in yogic structure – let us continue our journey by simplifying this intricate framework into two fundamental aspects - conscious mind and subconscious mind, subjective or objective mind, and logical and emotional mind.

You can imagine it as two types of minds synchronizing with each other. It's not about two entirely separate minds, but the spheres of activities co existing within the same mental space. So, how do they work in synchronization? Picture the conscious mind is the leader who gives command. In contrast, the unconscious mind is a follower that follows all the orders without questioning whether they are right or wrong. By understanding how they work in sync, we can begin to gain greater control over our thoughts and actions, leading to a more peaceful and fulfilling life.

Understanding the Conscious and Subconscious mind

Our conscious mind takes the front seat actively discerning what is good or bad for our life relying on the inputs it receives from our sensory organs, guiding our life on the right track. But what is the subconscious mind doing? Well, it operates behind the scene. The subconscious mind absorbs all the impressions the conscious mind is giving and starts working on them without questioning or validating the command. In simple terms, it begins to manifest the instruction from the conscious mind without asking any questions.

It's absolutely crucial to grasp that the subconscious mind is working 24x7, even when the conscious mind is sound asleep. It takes care of numerous bodily functions, such as blood circulation and breathing, all without any active engagement of conscious mind. This serves as the testament to the remarkable power and far-reaching impacts that the subconscious mind exerts on our daily lives.

When harnessed effectively the subconscious mind possesses the remarkable ability to infuse our life with boundless joy and ecstasy. Yet, it's important to note that the subconscious mind works for both good and bad ideas alike. If you find yourself preoccupied with negative thoughts, be aware that your subconscious mind will faithfully bring them to life. It can manifest pain, and unhappiness. The fascinating thing about the subconscious mind does not question or doubt; it simply accepts. So, if negative thoughts sink into the subconscious mind, it will accept them as true and create conditions, experiences, and events that will produce rejection, failure, frustration, and sadness.

Imagine your subconscious mind as fertile soil, ready to receive the seeds sown by your conscious mind. Whatever seeds you sow, whether good or bad, will grow, and you will get the fruit of the seeds you sowed. Thus, if you seek to alter the outcomes in your life, it all begins with the fundamental change in how you utilize your conscious mind.

Our subconscious mind operates based on a simple yet profound principle: the Law of belief. It acts as a bridge transforming wisdom from the universal intelligence to our conscious intellect. Visionaries, those who understand the working of mind, know how to make use of both the conscious and subconscious mind effectively. They use affirmations such as "I am in control. You follow me religiously." This reinforces the idea that the subconscious mind is subject to the conscious mind.

Unleashing the Power of the subconscious mind

Have you ever wondered why some people seem to effortlessly achieve health, wealth, and success while others struggle even when opportunities abound? The answer lies in the programming of their subconscious minds.

Our subconscious mind is like the master key that can unlock any door in our lives. But to take advantage of this incredible power, we first need to realize its potential. Think of it like a tiny seed that, when given the right conditions, can grow into a vast and thriving banyan forest. Or like a single atom that, when harnessed, can unleash an enormous amount of energy.

By programming our subconscious minds towards success, we are essentially creating a blueprint for the life we desire. This involves the deliberate selection of our thoughts, beliefs, and visualizations by creating a peaceful and harmonious environment within ourselves. When this new blueprint takes shape, our subconscious mind will automatically work towards making it a reality.

And the best part? Our subconscious mind operates tirelessly to achieve our goals, using all of its resources to bring our desires to life. Weather we seek improved health, greater success, or heightened happiness, we can trust in our subconscious mind's unwavering dedication to manifest our goals.

In short, when we assume command of our subconscious mind and align it with our aspirations the possibilities become bondless. So, let's start the journey today by planting those seeds of success today and witness them grow into the thriving forests of our dream.

The significant influence of our subconscious mind on our physical well- being is evident in the placebo effect, which has been acknowledged since the 18th century, but it continues to amaze doctors and researchers to this day. It shows that the mind is a powerful tool in healing the body.

The placebo effect?

It is a fascinating phenomenon in which people experience real improvement after taking a fake or non-existent treatment. Researchers have found that the placebo effect can ease pain, fatigue, and depression, among other conditions. With a history spanning centuries, the placebo effect remains a captivating subject for both researchers and doctors alike.

In a recent survey, doctors tested the placebo effect on migraine patients. They divided the patients into two groups: Group A received actual medicine for migraine, while Group B was given sugar pills (placebos). Astonishingly, both groups reported similar levels of pain relief!

In another investigation, some participants were given a placebo while others received actual treatment. However, doctors told all participants about the side effects that the medicine could cause. Surprisingly, many of those who received placebo developed the same side effects as the patients who received actual treatment.

In a particularly fascinating study, doctors conducted a placebo bypass surgery on a heart patient. They brought the patient to the operating theater, administered anesthesia, and performed some superficial incision on the skin, as if performing the surgery. They then stitched the skin back and told the patient that he had undergone a successful bypass surgery. Astonishingly, his heart ailment began to improve, and after one year, the blood supply in his heart had reached 100%, indicating that his heart had fully recovered. This incredible case vividly illustrates the power of the mind to heal the body.

In another remarkable incident, a criminal facing execution became apprehensive and was brought to the hospital by the police. He pleaded for a painless death. The doctors suggested administering a lethal injection that would result in immediate death.

They agreed that a nurse would administer the injection at midnight. However, the doctors did not want to kill him, so they instructed the nurse to inject him with saline water instead. The nurse carried out her job that night and injected the saline this patient. To their surprise, the patient died on the spot. How did it happen? How could a saline injection cause death? This baffling occurrence demonstrates the power of the subconscious mind to manifest our beliefs and expectations.

In conclusion, the placebo effect shows that our minds have a significant influence on our bodies. What we believe and expect can shape our reality, emphasizing the importance of harnessing the power of our minds to attain healing and wellness.

Historic Evidences

From start of Olympic games in 1896 until the first half of 20th century, it was a common belief that it was impossible for a human to run a mile in less than 4 minutes. Even medical professionals believed that human anatomy was simply not built to achieve such a feat. However, everything changed on May 6th,1954 when Roger Bannister made this world record completing a mile in just below 4 minutes. He shattered this long-standing belief and made history.

Roger Bannister was disappointed by achieving 4th position in Olympic performer of 1500 meter in 1952. It was then he decided to achieve what everyone else believed was impossible-to run a mile in less than 4 minutes. He visualized it in his mind convincing his subconscious that it was possible, and then set out to make it happen.

On that fateful day in 1954, he could run the race of a mile in an astonishing 3minutes and 59.4 seconds.

What followed was truly remarkable. In the same year 24 other runners also broke the record and in the next year 235 more running achieved the same feat. Something had changed and it was not just the physical potential of humans.

In the last 60 years no one could do that. What changed? First, Roger Bannister convinced his subconscious mind by visualizing that it was possible and his subconscious made it happen. After that the whole word got convinced that human body is capable of doing it and today the world record for 1500 meter is 3minutes and 26 seconds. And 3 minutes and 51.38 seconds for a mile 3.

Roger Bannister's incredible achievement is not just a testament to his physical abilities but also to the power of the human mind. He showed us that with the right mindset and belief, we can accomplish the seemingly impossible. His legacy continues to inspire athletes and non-athletes alike, reminding us that we are capable of achieving greatness if we set our minds to it.

Train subconscious mind through your conscious mind

Self-suggestions have immense power. You can suggest to your subconscious that I am becoming happier day by day, moment by moment.

Every time you offer such suggestion, it sinks into the subconscious mind and conditions are manifested. Now you have to decide what advice to send to your subconscious mind, whether it is the suggestion of joy and peace or fear, worry, or anxiety. It's important to mention that your conscious mind acts as the gatekeeper. Whatever it believes, the subconscious mind accepts with unwavering faith and acts upon zealously. Whatever you sincerely need in your life, you should have subconscious conviction. Your conscious and subconscious minds must agree.

Consider the pursuit of wealth, for instance. Your subconscious mind always accepts the focus idea. In this endeavor the focused idea should be wealth, not poverty. Overcoming any mental conflict about financial targets can be achieved by regularly affirming your daily journey towards wealth. Start sending visuals and start depositing thoughts of prosperity, wealth and success from your conscious mind to your subconscious mind. It is the sustained power of your imagination that brings miraculous working powers to our subconscious mind. You will see that the latter will give you wealth with compound interest.

Take the example of daily struggle with the morning alarm, the solution might lie in communicating directly with your subconscious mind. Instead of grappling with the snooze drama, suggest your subconscious mind the precise time you want to wake up, before going to sleep and it will awaken you accordingly. The subconscious mind works independently of a clock. Applying this approach to other persistence issues allows you to overcome fear as there is nothing virtually impossible for the subconscious to manifest.

Ingredients of affirmation: When you give affirmation need three ingredients

    A) Positive words, concise choice

    B) Visualization

    C) Corresponding feeling

Positive words, concise choice:

Words for affirmation should be chosen positively and specifically. For example, if you say, I love apples. Your mind recognizes that you are specific to yourself. It also recognizes "love", which means you want or like something. But when it comes to "apples", it starts searching in your hard disc word resembling apple- red apple, green apple, Washington apple, apple watch, apple mac book, and so on- this needs to be clarified. The message is not clear to the subconscious mind. So be positive and specific while sending affirmations.

When you create affirmations, use words like "I am becoming" instead of "I have become" This way your conscious mind does not resist the idea because it aligns with your current reality. The message will only sink into the subconscious mind if the conscious mind is convinced.

Visualization: Whatever you need from the subconscious mind, you need to visualize it. Visualization has the extreme power to convenience the subconscious mind.

Anything you want, say health, wealth, a house, a car, or becoming an astronaut or journalist, you need to see yourself possessing those things or becoming the same personality. For instant, you want a red car. visualize driving that red car again and again, with its steering in your hand. Create a clear mental picture of it. And even keep the visuals of that car in front of your working seat. It powerfully convinces your subconscious mind to manifest it. You will find circumstances becoming favorable for you to get closer to buying that red color car you've envisioned

The corresponding feeling

Here, the critical point is that you consciously affirm and should feel at the same. Don't affirm it and then deny it after a few moments. It will neutralize the good you have established. Also, envy and jealousy act as a blocker to the flow of your wealth and success. Your desire is your prayer. It comes from the most profound need and reveals what you need in life. Calmly think over what you want. See it coming to fruition from this moment firmly and repeatedly.

Conscious Mind as a Guard:

Any message we want to send to our subconscious mind goes through the Conscious mind.

Once the logical mind is convinced about it, only then does the information sink into your subconscious mind. Once the information reaches the subconscious mind, it becomes a part of your belief system. So how can we program our subconscious mind by taking care of a conscious mind?

Here are few ideas to send a message to subconscious mind:

Child Mind: When a child is 4-5 years old, his conscious mind is almost inactive. In this age, whatever information they observe, listen or feel, smell or taste impacts the subconscious mind. The conscious mind filter is not fully developed. In this stage, whatever parents, relatives, or teachers teach them remains in their mind forever and it becomes part of your life. For example, if a child is told that becoming wealthy is difficult and survival is tough. This belief or sanskara will remain with them and they may struggle in their pursuit of wealth. Conversely, if they are encouraged and told that they are great persons and they can achieve anything in life, they will develop a winning attitude as the subconscious mind will make them do great things.

Strong Logics: If any information is logically proven, means convenient for our conscious mind to think logically. In that case, our conscious mind gets satisfied and it does not restrict the info and that information goes to our subconscious mind. Think of it: When something just make sense, your conscious mind goes Aha! and let it go in without any barrier. Once it goes into the subconscious mind, it becomes your belief system and subconscious mind starts working on it.

Repetition of message: When some information is repeated again and again, at a point, it goes up to the subconscious mind. The conscious mind restricts it from passing through initially, but when it is repeated again and again logical mind accepts it as fact. It does not show much restriction and information can reach up to the subconscious mind. For example, if someone keeps telling you day after day that you are no good. After a while, you might start feeling a bit down and less effective. Why? Because that message has crossed the boundary of the conscious mind and found a home in your subconscious, where it starts to have its impact.

Similarly, if you keep hearing positive messages repetitively, it can improve your effectiveness, productivity and ability to tackle challenges with positive attitude,

Significant Personality: When someone important in your life shares something with you it directly goes to your subconscious mind, because you value their opinion very much. The conscious mind does not put any barrier because that person holds such significance for you and your conscious mind remained sidelined.

For instance, lessons taught by your parents and teacher remained with you throughout your life. Therefore, they have a profound influence on your thought process in your subconscious mind.

Emotions have power: When a message is associated with strong feelings, the logical mind gets distracted and takes a side seat- it doesn't restrict the information. Consider the example of a son who is with his father during his final moments. The father imparts some wisdom or shares his heart felt wishes with his son before passing away. The emotional weight of this message etches deep into son's conscious. The son may find that this message remains with him throughout his life, guiding his decisions, values and actions.

Hypnosis: It is a fascinating technique which can send direct messages to the subconscious mind. Hypnosis is derived from a Greek word "Hypnos" that means sleep. The word Hypnosis in Greek means Induced Sleep. In this technique, some experts make your conscious mind sleep with their skills and bypass the conscious logical mind. It involves guiding an individual's conscious mind into a unique stage that closely resembles the experience of being asleep. That is why hypnosis is used to program the subconscious mind. For example, when hypnotized, a person can be taken to a condition where he might vividly feel throbbing pain of a headache or even believe he is experiencing a nosebleed.

Sensory-rich language: Sensory rich language is like a magic carpet to your subconscious, bypassing the logical mind. It's a language painted with vivid pictures, resonate sounds and deep emotions It's not words; it's an experience that engages your senses.

Picture this: "It's early morning and I am strolling in a nearby garden. The air is crisp. And red color roses are in full bloom, painting the landscape with bright lively shades. The due on petals sparkle like pearls catching the first rays of sunlight. As I take a deep breath, the sweet fragrance of roses wraps around me like a warm huge that I enjoy with closed eyes. When I open my eyes, I am surrounded by endless bed of red roses, a breathtaking sight."

Can you feel the allure of the red rose beds and enchanting fragrance through these lines?

I aim not to tell you about roses but to make you feel the soft petals and inhale the fragrance deeply. It is a testament to the great impact words can have on our perception about the word around us.

Clarity of vision

There must be a definite idea in mind coupled with the certainty that there is a solution to the problem. The infinite universal intelligence within your subconscious mind holds the answer. Once you've formed a clear conclusion in your conscious mind, and are steadfast in your beliefs, your subconscious gets to work.

Realize the extreme potential of subconscious mind and always transmit positive signals through your conscious thoughts. You have power to shape your world. Consider your subconscious as tool – it can either be your greatest ally if programmed positively or your own adversary through negative self- talk.

What matters most is not what others tell you but what you tell yourself!

DO IT YOURSELF

1. How does the subconscious mind work?

2. Does the subconscious mind segregate excellent and bad ideas for you?

3. Name ten good mental foods (positive ideas) you would like to give to your mind.

4. How do self-suggestions get manifested?

5. How can you reduce your efforts for max output?

THE INNER WORLD

A quest within

"To those who conquered themselves, the will is a friend. But it is the enemy of those who have not found the self within them"

-Bhagwat Geeta

"If we know the divine art of concentration, if we know the divine art of meditation, if we know the divine art of contemplation, easily and consciously we can unite the inner world and the outer world."
-Sri Chinmoy

Senses are limited to the external world:

Most of us are born with five senses. We live a life based on what our senses tell us. These senses are essential for us to see, feel, smell, hear and taste the external physical world. However, it is important to realize that these sensory organs don't provide us insight into our inner selves. For example, we cannot see with our eyes what is going on within our stomachs

An ant crawling on our skin can be felt, but we can't feel what is happening inside our bodies. Although these five senses are essential for survival, they alone cannot foster internal development. One can get some motivational force from outside, and its effect will last for a limited period. But true and lasting motivation emanates from within.

The seeds of self-development sprout from your own awareness and consistent efforts. Your joy and misery comes from within. Establishing a stable foundation becomes imperative. If you strive, you can evolve yourself in whichever way you want.

Prioritize Self-Management

In the era of Technology, we have crafted a world of comfort, yet the need of the hour is for us to find comfort within ourselves. While we have developed attention to the external, the world within often remains overlooked. If we turn our focus to our inner selves, we can shape our world as we desire. In our pursuit of life goals, setting higher and higher targets we often lose the peace mind.

In the corporate ladder engineers, MBAs, accountants start their professional journeys and continue climbing the ladder to the status of General Manager or Vice president or the CEO. However, as one continues to climb up the corporate ladder, the magnitude of responsibilities grows, leading to heightened stress and intense discomfort. It reaches a tipping point where individuals perceive life a challenging ordeal. In the corporate circle, it's often remarked that as you climb higher, the oxygen level drops significantly. This stifling environment begins to affect both, health and relationship, ultimately robbing them of peace of mind. The greater the victory, the further we find ourselves from joy and happiness. Indeed, comfort may increase. But there comes a point, where it ceases to bring enjoyment and instead becomes a necessity.

What is the fun in attaining this success if you are not enjoying this brief life of yours in the universe?

Why are we suffering with our success?

This happens because we aim to manage our big team (the outer world) without giving any attention to managing our inner world.

Nurturing inner strength is like laying the groundwork for a fulfilled life. It involves simple yet powerful practices, including:

- Cultivate awareness and emotional balance
- Practice self-discipline and focus on what truly matters
- Stay in present and appreciate the now
- Tap into nature's wisdom and universal intelligence
- Foster gratitude and indulge in selfless giving
- Continuously choose happiness in your daily life.

These fundamental principles and practices will be further explored in the upcoming sections of this book, delving into the deeper aspects of each. As we journey together through these chapters, you'll gain valuable knowledge and tools to navigate your inner world and unlock its full potential.

Observe your thoughts

The more effortless you become; more the body and mind start functioning at their best. The human mind is capable of handling this outside world when it is joyful and finds bliss within. Clarity is the key for optimal mental functioning. Every human deserves a life filled with pleasant experiences. All renowned personalities have achieved greatness by managing their inner worlds.

Avoid attempting to control your thoughts for specific achievement. The nature of the human mind is such that resisting a particular thought often leads to its persistence. For instance, try not to think of a monkey and your mind immediately brings forth the image.

This happens because the mind doesn't understand prohibiting words like don't, never, or can't. It will immediately jump to the thought without these words.

As we explore further into intricacies of mind let us ponder on the concept of controlling the mind with sheer will power. Can your mind be mastered through strong determination? Is will power the ultimate answer to controlling the mind? The answer is a clear no. While your willpower may hold it for some time, but willpower will be defeated by the law of nature.

The most effective way to train your mind is to be friendly with yourself. When you are joyful, your body and mind cooperate at the best level. Talent only is not enough, the synergy between body and mind is essential for you to feel at your best. Your personal best should serve you; it may not be the best in the world.

At times overflow of thoughts can lead to a sense of unease. How to stop this influx of thoughts? It's simple-Pay attention to your thoughts. What kind of thoughts occupies your mind? Decide to choose happiness, that's true. Keeping oneself happy is a conscious decision by choice. Slowly you will be moving towards a state of ecstasy and thoughts that bring bliss and joy will start following. You will master the process gradually.

One way to achieve reaching heights where the mind experiences moments of tranquility, free from thoughts, allowing for pure observation is through making Yoga a way of life.

Enjoy present moments

Often, we find ourselves entangled in the intricate threads of vivid sense of memory and anticipation of the future. Inadvertently, we forget the beauty of present. This very today can turn into a gloomy yesterday or show the seeds of a blissful tomorrow.

Our suffering often stems from the haunting echoes of past adversities, or the anxiety about what tomorrow might bring. We keep recycling the hidden memories and based on the information, start painting a picture of the future. In this thought process, which I call the "diarrhea of the brain", we kill our present.

Yet the present is a beautiful gift bestowed upon us by nature urging us to be appreciated. If you start consciously enjoying the present moment, you can effortlessly achieve your goals and everything will naturally fall into place.

Compulsive reaction Vs. Conscious response

The domain of inner world unveils the complex dynamics that shape our responses to external stimuli. Our inside balance helps us know when to quickly react and when to think carefully. It's important not to delay decisions as they might become impulsive later on. Once it becomes compulsive, it won't bring joy to anyone.

In the face of different situations, our instinct is often to react immediately. However, reacting impulsively may not yield the most optimal outcome. Every problem presents an opportunity for the best possible response, one that requires thoughtful consideration.

Reacting is a manifestation of our emotions taking the lead. We cannot think of the best possible response under the influence of our anger or any other emotion. Recognizing this, it is in our best interest to cultivate a mindset of response rather than reaction.

Reacting hastily can lead to significant complication. Therefore, in the presence of numerous stimuli, we have to learn how to respond. It is possible only when you are stable from the inside. Rather than asking "Why did it happen to me", it is more powering to enquire. "How should I deal with it". Learn this master stroke not to react but to respond.

Life seldom presents ideal situations. There is always some kind of negativity that prevails in every circumstance. The difference lies in our choice – whether to respond with wisdom or succumb to wounds. By continuously choosing to respond instead of react we conserve our energies, maintain stability and cultivate wisdom in navigating life's challenges.

Self-discovery: Who I am?

As per the Hindu mythology the there exists a young sage named Bhrigu, the son of Varuna Rishi. One day Bhrigu approaches his father and asks, "Father, I want to know who I am" The wise Varuna tells his son, "Go and meditate to find the answer."

Bhrigu returns to his meditation, comes back and says, "I have realized that I am the body" Vauna responds, "No, you need to explore further. Meditate more and then tell me". Bhrigu goes back, meditates again and returns to tell, "I am the vital energy." Varun rejects this finding, "No, that is not true. Energy has movements and it keeps on changing. It is also the object of your perception. So go back and continue your meditation."

After another round of meditation, Bhrigu realizes something and comes back to his father "I am the intellect (buddhi)." he says. This time again, Varuna responds saying, "No, you are not. You can sharpen your intellect, blunt it, it is constantly changing, so it's also the object of your perception." Rishi Varuna again suggests Bhrigu to deep-dive into meditation and try to find himself.

This time Bhrigu goes into deep meditation and realizes something. He asks his father, "Am I the ultimate bliss and ecstasy?" Varuna acknowledges that Bhrigu is getting closer to the essence of his being. He explains that Bhrigu is an extreme power (Atman), a consciousness, a part of universal intelligence that operates through the body, intellect and energy."

Varuna clarifies that the body, energy, and intellect belong to Bhrigu, but he is not identified with them. Bhrigu is their owner, operating through them to perform activities. Varuna emphasizes that one should not identify oneself as the body or mind, rather one is an absolute part of the greater universal intelligence.

Bhrigu's journey of self-discovery through meditation teaches a great lesson: While possessions may belong to you, they do not define you. Instead, you are the extreme, absolute part of greater universal intelligence. Upon realizing this fundamental truth, universal intelligence flows through your intellect, becoming evident in your vision and fostering internal stability. This new found understanding significantly enhances your ability to achieve extraordinary heights in any field of life.

DO IT YOURSELF

1.Try to explain yourself a situation you didn't react but responded.

2. Do you take out few minutes daily for inner talks?

3. Practice stopping and checking yourselves if you are truly fully involved in the present.

4. Can you achieve inner word contentment through the five senses?

5. Do you know yourself?

PEACE

&

HAPPINESS

Nurturing Tranquility

"Happiness is a state of mind that has nothing to do with the external world"

-Bhagwat Geeta.

*"We can never obtain peace in the outer
world until we make peace with
ourselves."*

-Dalai Lama

Peace doesn't come from calm surroundings. Peace means remaining calm, focused in the middle of all mayhem, chaos, noise and difficulties.

A peaceful mind creates a happier person.

Can we say - Peace is happiness at rest and happiness is peace in motion?

Pleasure and Peace:

Today we are the most comfortable generation humanity has ever known. Despite countless conveniences, peace remains an elusive phantom slipping through our hands like a fleeting wisp of smoke. A void or sense of emptiness within always keeps on disturbing our minds. Many of us try to seek peace from our physical comforts. We make life more and more comfortable for the sake of peace. While some tend to overindulge in many activities to get rid of the emptiness, some seek peace in activities such as going to gyms, movies, swimming pools, temples of bars, and restaurants, while others travel to change the environment, but all in vain.

Happiness lies in peace, it's not in mere pleasure!

In our search of happiness, we often turn to pleasure. Pleasure is an inferior substitute for happiness. Excess of pleasure will increase the emptiness within. While it may offer temporary respite, no physical or external means can truly fulfill the emptiness within.

Today human has developed technology. Now with AI the technology itself is doing advanced innovations. This advancement has brought a world of unparalleled conveniences and comforts. But this technology has also made humans restless, finding comfort but lacking peace of mind. In ancient days we aimed to make arrangements for our stomachs and focus on survival. With time human race evolved and survival became easier.

So, in earlier days, the only issue that concerned us was how to make our stomachs full. But now, hundreds of problems bother us. Turns out, an empty stomach may bring one problem, but a full stomach can bring you countless more.

Our five senses can make us realize the world around us, but they cannot tell us about our inner selves. We need to take the help of our self-consciousness to know our inner selves. The fact is that permanent peace and calmness can be generated only from the inner you, not from the external world. Do you know why ancient yogis in India used to leave the physical pleasure and mediate for years on the peak of mountains? Does this mean that they did not like the joy of life? The answer is they preferred a more profound and lasting form of happiness, the inner one. After attaining the stage of calmness, through self-discipline and meditation, the whole world became immaterial for them as they tasted absolute joy, self-realization, inner peace and the spiritual enlightenment.

An essential requirement and not an ultimate goal

I find peace sitting beside a peaceful blue lake. The standstill lake reflects the calm within me. I feel a deep sense of tranquility connecting me to nature's serenity. Yet, throwing a small stone ruins the stability of the lake's water and I watch as ripples spread outward, causing tiny disturbances on the once-calm surface. I realize that essence of peace lies not just in the stillness of lake but in cultivating the inner sense of calm that can endure the inevitable disturbances of daily life. I cherish the lakes beauty and the clam it awakens in me.

Ironically, the fundamental nature of life is becoming so complicated that people cannot be at peace with them. Some gurus have started saying that finding peace is the ultimate goal of life. This is not true at all. As being peaceful from within is a fundamental prerequisite for accomplishing anything significant in life. Peace is a basic requirement for a fulfilled life, not the ultimate goal.

Involve but not entangle

It cannot be tackled by doing something physically. It's your psychology; it'll come from within.

Let us try to get the root cause of that emptiness from within. Reflect into your inner self, and genuinely ask yourself for, "why am I suffering?"

The core issue lies in how we attach ourselves to many things. It's natural that many thoughts come to our minds. There is no issue with thought. You must have thought of a car, house, shirt, hair style, or something else, which is absolutely fine. However, problems start when we start identifying ourselves with these objects. There is nothing inherently wrong about having a car. If you consider the car to be a machine available to you that enables you to travel comfortably and save time, it's reasonable and sensible thing to think, but what we do is we start developing excessive attachment and emotional identifications with the car or any possession.

We start breeding ideas like "My car is better than his," "I love my car," or "I can only go in my car" etc. This in most cases leads to a distorted mindset and unhealthy perspective. We need to learn to engage with material things without entangling ourselves with them and without identifying ourselves with those objects.

We need not necessarily go to the mountains for the realization of ourselves instead we need to learn the art of remaining engaged with materialistic things while maintaining a sense of detachment with them. Whether name or fame, position, or any other thing - Don't get identified with it, because it is not yours and it is not valid. It is essential to fulfill your responsibility towards your family, earning a living and providing good education, food and other resources. We must take care of our parents and even society. Simultaneously we must avoid over attachment to these materialistic things. The attachment will become the cause of worry and will keep you away from happiness.

Bhagavad Gita Chapter 2, Verse 71 (BG 2.71)

"That one who gives up all material desires and lives free from greed, proprietorship, and egoism, attains perfect peace".

We need to go from lies to truth. Once we identify with anything, it creates a storm in our minds and our ship starts sinking. You move from reality to a world of hallucination which in the long term becomes dangerous to your own life. Once you are closer to reality, you can avoid unnecessary complications in your life. Our self-consciousness will keep us surfing over the waves of a materialistic world.

Bhagavad Gita Chapter 2, Verse 70 (BG 2.70):

"Just as the ocean remains undisturbed by the incessant flow of water from rivers merging into it, likewise the sage, who is unmoved despite the flow of desirable objects all around him, attains peace, not the person who strives to satisfy desires."

Satisfied or successful

Everybody wants to be successful in life. Now success has a different meaning to different people. In fact, the notion of success varies significantly from person to person. For some earning a lot of money, a big house, a luxury car, and a big bank balance is success, while others feel thriving when they have better social status and respect. For many of us success is comparative to others. Some relate it to karma, whereas some seek success in living a contented life.

Once again, as long as we are synchronized with nature and follow its laws, we can lead a satisfying life. As it is mentioned in Bhagwat Geeta, the great Indian epic, we are born with empty hands and will depart in the same way. Despite this truth we try to find peace in the possession of materialistic things. We complete one desire the 2nd arises. We achieve the 2nd the next appears and this phenomenon continues till the end of this journey through life. We don't find absolute satisfaction. Slowly, it becomes evident that there's something else which can give us peace of mind and satisfying life. A satisfying life is always better than a mere successful life.

Moreover, we often frame life as a constant struggle between me versus the universe. We view it as "Me vs. my neighbor", "me vs. my colleague," "me vs. my family/friend," and "me vs. the world". In other words, it is a self-centered attitude. However, a paradigm shift is essential. It is not universe vs. me. Rather "I am the universe", or the "universe is within me."

Fear of the future and painful past

Our mental baggage often ties us to the past or traps us in worries about the future, leading to feelings of anxiety and emptiness. We accumulate conditioning over time—beliefs and ideas that can isolate us and drain our inner peace. However, when we free ourselves from the weight of these past memories, beliefs, and ideas, we begin to experience true inner tranquility. Recognizing that our fears about the future are merely projections influenced by past experiences allows us to release these anxieties. By embracing the present moment, we can let go of unnecessary fears and find peace in the here and now. In the present, suffering does not exist; it is a space of calm and clarity.

Reaction Vs Responsiveness

Never react to a situation; always respond to it. Let me illustrate this with an example.

A fire once broke out in a multistory building. As soon as the occupants became aware of the danger, panic spread rapidly. Some people instinctively bolted toward the stairs, hoping to escape. Others, thinking quickly, grabbed water canisters in an attempt to extinguish the flames. Many dialed the fire brigade, seeking professional help, while some wrapped themselves in wet blankets to avoid inhaling smoke. Amidst the chaos, a few individuals were so overwhelmed that they became paralyzed with fear, unable to do anything but cry out for help. Tragically, some were so terrified that they jumped out of windows, losing their lives in the process.

The situation was the same for everyone—a fire in the building. Yet, it's striking to see how differently people responded to the same threat. Some took reckless, life-threatening actions, while others made more measured decisions. This underscores the importance of learning to respond to situations with calm and clarity rather than reacting impulsively out of fear. Responding allows us to think clearly and take actions that can lead to safety and resolution, while reacting may lead to unnecessary harm.

Situations are mostly not in our hands and keep on changing. Good things and bad things happen to us without our permission. But it is our response to the situation that makes or breaks us. I have often heard people saying, "He made me crazy" or "I don't want to see his/her face again". But the fact is no one can make me suffer without my permission. If somebody tries to provoke me or insult me, I have the power to decide consciously not to react. I can exhaust their efforts by keeping calm and peaceful. It is possible indeed.

The critical thing to note here is to always be conscious about your response to the situation. Merely, with your response, you can make your life hell or heaven. No situation or individual can make your life difficult without your permission. Human being does not mean suffering. Instead, being human is great.

Happiness is a state of mind. I can decide to keep myself happy for today, tomorrow and every next moment. Pain and suffering are two different things. Pain is natural, but suffering is our state of mind due to pain. I can very well decide not to suffer due to pain.

Choose happiness:

We need to be conscious for taking responsibility for our own life. It is my life and I am responsible for it. I don't give my power of attorney to anyone. Nobody can make me angry without my consent. If we look at situations from a cause-and-effect point of view. External things are the effect, not the cause. Your thoughts are causes which produce unique effects. Choose happiness because you will never get ideal situations in life. Some things will always be out of your control. It depends on you whether you choose to be wise or wounded.

Make your decisions once the mind is calm.

We need to learn to be calm in every situation. With this steady state of mind, we should analyze the situation. Our inner consciousness gives us solutions in this relaxed state. Following that pure and positive inner voice, we can respond to the situation. This way of working will lead us to the most incredible heights.

If we jump to conclusion in an excited state, chances of making wrong decisions increase and so does the suffering from their consequences. These sufferings destroy our peace and we continue to endure them in our life.

The decision we take today determines our tomorrow - The quality of your life quality today is a result of decisions you made in the past.

Therefore, you should make decisive choices and move ahead instead of lingering on with some issues. Sometimes we make mistakes while taking decisions: however, it is essential to learn fast from them and take the next decision with previous experience. Don't let the fear of mistake paralyze you into indecisiveness. It is proven that decisions taken with a peaceful mind are always better than those made with an excited state of mind.

Never make long-term decisions in a state of anger or heightened emotion. Instead, approach decision-making with a calm mind, and avoid getting caught up in the pursuit of perfection. If you insist on gathering every bit of information or wait for the perfect conditions, you may never make a decision at all. Consider this: if you keep searching for the perfect spouse, someone who meets every single one of your criteria, there's a 100% chance you'll remain single indefinitely. Perfection is elusive, and in reality, it's our ability to accept and work with imperfections that leads to fulfilling relationships and sound decisions.

Allow you to fail and bounce back.

Worrying about tomorrow and being consumed by sadness over past memories instead of focusing on today is the biggest mistake most of us make. Also, nothing is permanent in this world. Things are either temporarily permanent or permanently temporary. If something has gone wrong, let it be. Bounce back with more energy, enthusiasm and better spirit this time.

Failures are stepping stones on our journey, guiding us toward growth and improvement. We should embrace them, as they often teach us more valuable lessons than success ever could. If you truly want to gain deep insights into any field, focus on reading, listening to, and watching failure stories rather than just success stories. Failures reveal the challenges, missteps, and hard-earned lessons that can illuminate the path forward, helping you avoid similar pitfalls and better prepare for the future.

Failures are beautiful and they are necessary for our success. They make our foundation strong. Anything which gives us experience gives us wonderful learning, and prepares us for the future. Then, how it can be a bad thing? Never feel like a victim after experiencing failure. We should transform our attitude from "Why me" to "Try me." Always ask the universe to test and challenge you. Consider these challenges as opportunity for growth and self-improvement. Take chances, find solutions and keep on moving with peace of mind. Don't keep blaming yourself for past mistakes. Instead, use them as opportunities for learning and then move further. Being more conscious of both the inside and outside of yourself is crucial. Self-talk pays a vital role in realizing this fact. We must make time for ourselves, especially for self-talk on daily basis to keep ourselves on track and aligned with our goals.

Money matters

We feel happy as zeros in our bank balance increase over time. Many of us keep accumulating massive wealth, even at the cost of our health. However, ultimately, we might not be able to fully enjoy that wealth owing to weak health. I am not at all against earning money. Money is undeniably essential for survival and social security in today's world, at the same time, we should not spend our whole life chasing money. Making money should not be the only target of our life; we should strive to find a balance and understand how much is enough. We should aim to make this journey more cheerful, and vibrating not only for us but also for the betterment of our society at large. There is so much more to experience and appreciate in this universe beyond the pursuit of material world.

Strong opinion about others and yourself

Don't keep trying to change people. Instead of changing everything around you, it's better to bring positive change within your area of influence. It's like the saying goes, "It's better to wear slippers than carpet the whole earth."

A person cannot live alone in this world; he/she needs others to fulfill life. However, the other side of the story is that humans find it hard to get along with others. They might dislike someone because of their thoughts or looks - a wife might not get along with her husband, mother-in-law, boss or neighbor because they think differently. This difference may lead to negative feelings and even wishing harm upon them.

Mind the law of nature: You are polluting your conscious and subconscious mind with the poison of ill feelings about someone. This toxicity is inside you, so it will kill you only, not the other. Often, we mistakenly feel that by consuming this poison others will suffer. In reality, it's going to harm only you and not them.

We often dislike others because they are not like us. Why should they be like you? It's important to understand that nature has made everyone differently. Everybody is unique and nobody is flawless in this world. Let's shift our attention to what went wrong instead of who made it bad. If you are continuously focusing on a person's mistakes, you will never understand his point of view. Try not to form a strong opinion about others and yourself.

In his book "The 7 Habits of Highly Effective People" Stephen Covey emphasizes a valuable principle – "First listen to understand and then aim to be understood." Many a times we pretend to listen only to react quickly, but it's important to genuinely listen with empathy and gratitude to understand.

Empathy is like stepping into someone else's shoes. It means thinking, "If I were in the situation what would my experience be?" This way, you understand others better and you don't generate ill will with this understanding and you move on the path of your inner peace without much effort.

We should accept the fact: What happened, happened and could not have unfolded differently. Many of us find it tough to accept this leading to a loss of mental peace. There is no need to carry guilt for past life. Nothing happens by chance, even if it sounds dramatic. Everything happens for a reason. Remember, the basic rule is to live today without sinking deep into the past or painting an overly idealized, beautiful picture of the future. Living and observing in the present is the right way to achieve peace.

What will People say?

Other People's opinions of you are none of your business. They possess the right to their view point and you have the right to ignore it as well. Remember, don't seek gratification from your praise or feel disheartened by blame.

A person who is always balanced in his approach will live in peace. One should not get over excited when life is in favor and at the same time remain undeterred when challenges arise.

Remain balanced and focused on your aim. People keep on changing their opinion. If you are doing good, they'll ask "How are you?" When you expect their help in a difficult situation, the same people will say, "Who are you?" So don't bother about their opinion.

Happiness is the harvest of a calm mind. So, our aim should be to achieve peace in all situations by keeping our cool. Then only we can progress to cultivate our emotions and energies leading us towards the path of success.

The key is in your thoughts.

Nothing is accomplished without desire. You must sincerely desire to experience happiness. Desire is like a wish with wings made of imagination and faith. Imagine the fulfillment of your desire, truly feel its reality, and it will eventually become a reality.

On the flip side, if you constantly dwell on fear, failure, worry, anger, and hate, you will inevitably become depressed and unhappy. Remember this: your life is shaped by your thoughts. Happiness cannot be bought with money alone. There are millionaires who are content, but there are also those who are deeply unhappy. Likewise, some people with modest resources find joy, while others with similar means struggle to feel satisfied. The same goes for relationships—some married individuals are fulfilled, while others are not, and some singles are joyful while others feel unfulfilled. In a nutshell, the key to happiness lies within your thoughts and emotions. How you perceive your life, not your circumstances, ultimately determines your happiness.

As per words of Sadhguru, "When our body becomes pleasant, we term it **Healthy**. When it becomes more pleasant, we call it **Peace**. When our emotions become pleasant, we call it **Joy**. When it becomes more pleasant, we call it **Compassion.** When our energy becomes pleasant, we call it **Bliss** and when it becomes more pleasant, we call it **Ecstasy**. And when our surroundings become pleasant, we call it a **Succes**s."

DO IT YOURSELF

1. Is peace your ultimate goal in your life? Justify your answer

2. Do you agree that peace of mind doesn't depend on the situation? If yes, why?

3. What is your opinion on - human beings being a slave in situations?

4. How do you identify yourselves? Think of yourself as having no identity.

5. Explain any situation where you took a decision with a calm mind and got very good results.

THE MOTHER NATURE

Pristine Planet

"All works are being done by the energy and power of nature, but due to delusion of ego, people assume themselves to be the doer."

- Bhagavad Geeta.

"There is pleasure in the pathless woods, there is rapture in the lonely shore, there is a society where none intrudes, by the deep sea, and music in its roar; I love not Man the less, but Nature more."

-Lord Byron.

Nature, the perfect Creator

Imagine yourself in a serene backdrop, on a rock that sits under a tree outside a hut. You're in the midst of a valley, in the lap of nature. As far as your eyes can see, there are huge green landscapes. A river is passing by with melodious music in its flow. Colorful fishes are swimming in the water, numerous blossoming buds and beautiful flowers peeking from the bushes with their wonderful fragrance attracting honey bees that continuously hover on them. Birds are chirping, a white rabbit is pounding up and down, peacocks are dancing nearby. A cool breeze is tickling you now and then. A baby tortoise approaches your feet slowly. Clouds are passing over your head. Multicolored butterflies trying to talk to you softly, tall trees making the gateway: Many of them are full of fruits bowing down to earth. A mother bird feeds her infant in her nest on the branch of a tree.

You look up to see the spectrum of rainbows and birds flying in a row in the vast blue sky. You feel so comfortable in the sun's warmth when it comes out of clouds intermittently. Your body and mind is filled with wonderment when you exclaim – wow!

And to your surprise, Mother Nature responds through the valley and sends back the eco – Wow! Wow! Wow! Mother Nature is thrilled to see her son filled with joy!

We call nature a mother as every human has come from nature. The Creator has created this world with such perfection that we cannot even imagine. Despite the advancement of science and technology, we still need help understanding this creation. We can utilize what nature has granted us but can't fully comprehend even the simplest of its aspects. The universe contains countless of planets, millions of galaxies and starts. Tell me, how are the many planets revolving in this universe without any collision? How are the timings perfectly calculated for the earth? How does the sun rise, shine and set in perfect time. Countless varieties of flowers adorn the planet. The water cycle, the air cycle, every aspect functions in harmony. We enjoy different changing seasons on earth: winter, summer, spring, and autumn.

What does this all prove? The tall green mountains, snow-capped peaks, giggling rivers, stunning glaciers and musical waterfalls along with calm desert, the deep, wonderful sea and its treasures, rich forests, the blue sky and, and a self-sustaining ecosystem are enough to prove that nature has created everything in a perfectly balanced way. Human creation can never surpass the brilliance of nature.

"Look deep into nature, and then you will understand everything better," Albert Einstein.

According to Hindu mythology, the human body is made of five tattvas (elements), namely Prithvi (earth), Jal (water), Vayu (air), Aakash (sky), Agni (fire) and at the end of life our body gets dissolved back into these five elements. Made of it, we naturally get attracted towards nature and all its elements. Nature has the ultimate creativity. Just think of the blossoming flowers, dancing fish, birds chirping, the rising sun, and the full moon. Try to understand the cool breeze, the dancing peacock, the roaring lion, the swimming swan, the lotus in filth, the giant elephant, the tall giraffe, the moving ant, the scrolling snake, and running tiger – How beautifully is everything made.

Our entire life is too short to fully comprehend nature's laws and discipline. We need to enjoy and appreciate nature rather than attempting to control and overcome its natural process. By getting closer to nature, we can experience its unique way of rejuvenating our spirits.

But the sad part is that we are continuously abusing nature in the name of our development. Many a times, we think of ourselves vs. nature. Yet, everybody's survival is possible once we gel with the universal system. Nature is like a mother who knows what is best for her child.

Human creation Vs. Nature's creation

There is enough for everyone in nature for one's needs but not for everyone's greed. Abusing nature and natural resources has made our life meaningless. Nature has its ways and means to restore things to position against human desire, which sometimes becomes disastrous. In the name of development, humans have shaved the planet, removing forests, stopping rivers by building bridges – We kept on interfering and trying to tame nature for our benefits. We cross our limits destroying nature.

As a result, our rivers are dying, they are polluted and now lack of oxygen. This water has become poison for its inhabitants. We produce an enormous amount of CO_2 and other harmful gasses through various activities which lead to air pollution. When water and air are polluted, they affect every aspect of human life, giving rise to illness and health issues. Furthermore, environmental pollution disturbs natural cycles. Global warming is another problem from the same cause.

The depletion of Ozone layer leaves living creatures exposed to dangerous ultraviolet rays. It poses further risk to health and eco system. The impact of human development action is evident in melting glaciers, and rising sea levels. The earth's temperature is gradually increasing each year and natural resources are depleting at an alarming rate. In addition to this our topsoil is slowly becoming infertile, posing significant challenges for agriculture and food production

People often adopt new means of comfort without keeping in mind the balance of nature. For instance, cutting mountains to make new roads and widening them is resulting in dangerous landslides in the hilly regions. Constructing dams across rivers for irrigation or electricity production can unintentionally lead to floods. Indiscriminate tree-cutting for building houses, roads, and commercial structures contributes to air pollution and rising temperatures.

The pursuit of comfort and pleasure has lead to the production of various consumer goods which has resulted in air and water pollution. This indicates that much of what we create is artificial or unnatural. It has disrupted the delicate balance maintained by Mother Nature. Once the natural balance is disturbed, we invite natural disasters in the form of pollution, storms, floods, rain without season, excessive heat, excessive cold, epidemics, pandemics, and so on.

We often neglect nature and think that this is our nature. With each passing generation human beings are getting away from mother nature and becoming more absorbed in comfort and convenience while losing discipline and balance in their lives. This repetitive dose of comfort and pleasure over a long period has a significant negative affect on our body, mind, psychology, and thought processes. Unfortunately, these harmful effects can become irreversible over time.

Most of the times, we try to find solutions to this sickness by medicine which again has chemicals which suppress the illness forcefully and give so many other (side) effects on our physical health and metal well-being.

Indeed, we find ourselves trapped in vicious cycle – we try to seek a pill for every ill. We must understand to come out of this endless cycle, we as a human society must delve deeper to address the root cause of our health issues. Many Lifestyle diseases like hypertension, high blood pressure, disabilities etc. can be effectively managed and even cured by embracing a more natural way of life and incorporating naturopathy particles. Nature has much to offer in terms of healing and promoting well beings.

Yoga in particular the best way to maintain good health keeps these diseases at a distance. It is a holistic approach not only to strengthen the body but to enhance mental and emotional well- being. Regular practice of Yoga helps us to maintain a balance between mind, body and spirit

Natural potential

Mother Nature is powerful: it birthed us and can keep us mentally and physically sound throughout our life until we eventually dissolve into it at the end of our life. Many studies have shown that a person remains happier living near nature. Nature rejuvenates us quickly and gives us strength and energy. It improves our immunity and teaches us discipline. It heals our body and mind in different ways. In a nutshell, this body and mind is a part of nature only. Therefore, humanity should learn to come closer to nature and develop technologies that gel with nature and natural laws.

Being in nature reduces stress.

It's clear that hiking or any physical activity can reduce stress and anxiety. But there's something about being in nature that may augment those impacts.

In a recent study in Japan, the participants were told to walk of equal length and difficulty in either a forest or an urban center. During the walk their heart rate variability, heart rate, and blood pressure were measured. Additionally, the participants also completed questionnaires about their stress levels, moods and many other psychological aspects.

The results of the study showed that those who walked in forests exhibited significantly lower heart rates and higher heart rate variability, indicating more relaxation and less stress and reported better moods and less anxiety as compared to those who walked in urban settings. The researchers concluded that being in nature had a positive effect on stress reduction, surpassing the benefits of exercise alone.

In another study, researchers in Finland found that urban dwellers who wander for as little as 20 minutes through an urban park or woodland reported significantly more stress relief than those who wandered in a city center.

The reasons for this effect are unclear, but scientists believe that we have evolved to be more relaxed in natural spaces.

In a classic laboratory experiment by Roger Ulrich of Texas A & M University with his colleagues, participants viewed a stress-inducing movie and were then exposed to color/sound videotapes depicting either natural or urban scenes. The results showed that participants who were exposed to natural scenes experienced much quicker, more complete recovery from stress than those who had been exposed to videos of urban settings.

These studies along with others provide evidence that being in natural spaces or even just looking out of a window onto a natural scene somehow soothes us and relieves stress.

2. Nature makes you happier and less brooding

Gregory Bratman of Stanford University has conducted a study proving evidence of nature's impact on our mood. In 2015, Bratman and his colleagues randomly assigned 60 participants to a 50-minute walk in either a natural setting or an urban setting. Before and after the walk, the participant's emotional state and cognitive measures were assessed.

The results showed that those who walked in nature experienced lower level of anxiety and rumination-which refers to focused attention on negative aspects of oneself, in comparison to the participants who walked in urban environments. Additionally, the natural walkers exhibited improved performance on memory tasks.

Rumination has been associated with the onset of depression and anxiety. The team used fMRI technology to look at brain activity. Participants had their brains scanned before and after their walks and were surveyed on self-reported rumination levels (as well as other psychological markers). The researchers controlled for many potential factors that might influence rumination or brain activity—for example, physical exertion levels as measured by heart rates and pulmonary functions.

Even so, participants who walked in a natural setting reported decreased rumination after the walk and showed increased activity in the subgenual prefrontal cortex, an area of the brain whose deactivation is affiliated with depression and anxiety—a finding that suggests nature may have substantial impacts on mood.

Bratman believes results like these must reach city planners and others whose policies impact our natural spaces. "Ecosystem services are being incorporated into decision-making at all levels of public policy, land use planning, and urban design, and it's very important to be sure to incorporate empirical findings from psychology into these decisions," he says.

3. Nature relieves attention fatigue and increases creativity.

Today, we live with ubiquitous technology designed to constantly pull our attention. Many scientists believe our brains were not made for this kind of constant information bombardment, which can lead to mental fatigue, overwhelm, and burnout. Thus, we often require "attention restoration" to get back to a normal, healthy state.

Strayer is one of those researchers. He believes being in nature restores depleted attention circuits, which can help us be more open to creativity and problem-solving.

"When you use your cell phone to talk, text, shoot photos, or whatever else you can do with your cell phone, you're engaging the prefrontal cortex and causing reductions in cognitive resources," he says.

In a 2012 study, Stayer and his colleagues showed that hikers on a four-day backpacking trip were able to solve significantly more puzzles that required creativity compared to a control group of people waiting to take the same hike. In fact, they solved 47 percent more puzzles to be precise.

Although other factors may account for these results such as the exercise or the camaraderie of being out together, previous studies have suggested that nature itself may play an important role. For example, a study published in psychological science found that nature's impact on attention restoration accounted for improved cognitive test scores among the participants.

This phenomenon may result from differences in brain activation as opposed to more urban settings, even for those who typically reside in urban environments.

This demonstrates that a natural setting helps restore attention, promoting a more open, meditative mindset. This kind of brain activity—sometimes referred to as "the default brain network" is associated with creative thinking, stays Staler.

4. Nature may help you to be kind and generous

In a series of experiments published in 2014, Juyoung Lee, the GGSC director Dacher Keltner, and other researchers at the University of California, Berkeley, investigated the potential impact of nature on the people's willingness to be generous, trusting, and helpful toward others. They were curious about the factors might influence this relationship.

As their study, the researchers exposed participants to varying level of subjective natural beauty (whose beauty levels were rated independently). They then observed how participants behaved playing two economics games: the Dictator Game and the Trust Game, which measure generosity and trust, respectively. The results were fascinating. Participants who were exposed to the more beautiful nature scenes, acted more generously and more trusting in the games than those who saw less beautiful scenes. These effects appeared to be linked to corresponding increases in positive emotion.

In another phase of the study, participants were asked to complete an emotional survey while sitting at a table where more or less beautiful plants were placed. Following this, participants were told that the experiment was over and they were free to leave, but that if they wanted to, they could volunteer to make paper cranes for a relief effort program in Japan. The number of cranes they made (or didn't make) was used as a measure of their 'pro-sociality' or willingness to help.

Results revealed that the presence of more beautiful plants significantly increased the number of cranes crafted by participants. Furthermore, this increase was, once again, attributed to positive emotion elicited by natural beauty. The researchers concluded that experiencing the beauty of nature increases positive emotions, positively inspiring awe, a feeling akin to wonder, with the sense of being part of something bigger than oneself. These positive emotions in turn lead to pro social behaviors.

Support for this theory is drawn from an experiment conducted by Paul Piff of the University of California, Irvine, and his colleague. In this study participants who spent just one minute glazing up at grove of very tall trees experienced measurable increases in awe.

Notably, they exhibited helpful behavior and approached moral dilemmas with greater ethical consideration as compared to the participants who spent the same amount of time looking up at a tall building

5. Nature makes you "feel alive."

Given all of these benefits to being out in nature, it's probably no surprise that something about nature makes us feel alive and vital. Being outdoors provides us with energy, boosts our happiness, helps us to relieve the everyday stress that comes with our busy lives, opens the door to creativity, and encourages kindness towards others.

The Ideal amount of nature exposure remains uncertain and there is no definitive answer. Nevertheless, Strayer points out that seasoned backpackers suggest a minimum of three days.

Also, it remains unclear how natures expose compare to other form of stress relief or attention restoration such as sleep and mediation. Strayer and Bratman empathize the need for much more careful research to tease out these effects before we come to any definitive conclusions.

Nevertheless, the research does suggest that nature plays a vital role to keep us psychologically healthy.

This is particularly reassuring, given that nature is freely available resource, easily accessible just by stepping outside our doors. Results like these should encourage us as a society to consider more carefully how we can preserve our wilderness and urban parks.

Nature doesn't need people, but people need nature

Nature doesn't rely on people but people depend on nature. The extent to which we are exploiting natural resources is a matter of great concern. Just imagine how nature would reclaim a city amended by people for years. In deed our connection to this earth is undeniable. In the end our bodies return to the soil providing valuable nourishment to the growth of plants and trees.

Our society's key features including political leaders, educationists, scientists, technologists, medical fraternity, industrialists, environmental advocates, lawyers and students all have a pivotal role to play to cultivate a deep sensitivity towards nature. In the classroom of Mother Nature there are countless lessons in creativity and ecology waiting to be learned. Nature's resilience and ability to sustain itself over eons serves as a remarkable model for existence of human kind.

With this mindset, let us pave the way for longer and profoundly meaningful lives.

DO IT YOURSELF

1. Do you need nature, or does nature need you?

2. Why do you feel comfortable when you are in nature?

3. When did you observe the power of nature in your experience?

4. Explain any moment when do desperately wanted nature around you.

5. Have you ever talked to any animal besides Humans? How was the experience?

THOUGHT PROCESS

&

OBSERVATION

Exploring the dynamics

"A man who sees action in inaction and inaction in action has understanding among men and discipline in all action he performs."

\- Bhagwat Gita

Eat, sleep, produce and die; that is what all animals accomplish in their lives. Humans, however are unique creatures gifted with evolved minds that set them apart. Our ability to think, imagine and visualize is what defines our experience.

Our thoughts shape our life. Action-oriented people with the correct positive mindset always have an edge over others in every field of life. Thinking is a powerful tool that allows us to plan, create and innovate. However, it's essential to remember that thinking alone can sometimes lead us to over analysis, hesitation or stress.

Observation on the other hand, is being fully in the present moment and absorbing the world around us. Through observation we can get valuable insight and knowledge that thinking alone might overlook.

In some situations, our thoughts may lead us astray, cloud us by biases or preconceptions. Observation in the other hand provides a deeper understanding and encourages open mindedness.

Churning the same data again and again

When we engage in thinking, we are essentially processing the data already stored in our brains. Over time we revisit the same data repeatedly which can lead to a repeating similar experience. The key point here is if we want different results, we need to input new data through fresh observations in our lives

Our conclusions, often shaped by past experiences may not always match with Nature or the Universe. Everybody has their own perspective and makes decisions based on their intelligence. But sometimes these decisions turn out to be wrong. This is when we realize the importance of expanding our horizon

Overthinking

Over thinking can be quite a burden. Our mind gets entangled in the intricate web of thoughts. We weave narratives which consume our attention. This process can give rise to negative thoughts, producing fear of the future and frightening us. Conversely, over-optimism can lead to excitement fueling our expectations. It's like riding an emotional rollercoaster with a constant stream of thoughts wearing us out and most times, we come back to square one.

On average, we have around fifty to sixty thousand thoughts per day and are grappled with issues. This overthinking can be linked to mental diarrhea. Just as physical diarrhea drains our energy and leaves us feeling helpless, mental diarrhea can sap our mental energy and leave us indecisive. Negative thoughts that enter our mind are like contaminated or undigested food in stomach; they often are the culprit.

So how do we recover from physical diarrhea? We stop eating first, purge our stomach and stay hydrated. Likewise for our mental diarrhea, we need to stop consuming those harmful thoughts. Try to keep your mind free of excessive thought and focus on observing the kind of thought that enters your mind. Let positivity flow through your minds just as you would hydrate your body with water.

Simply Observe

To achieve different results, we sometimes need to change our approach. But where does this new approach come from? Should we constantly seek new ideas? Not necessarily. Mere thinking alone does not change the outcome. To achieve fresh results, it's essential to shift from thinking to observing. What does it mean? It means living in the present. Embrace to live life as it unfolds. Just observe your thoughts as they are.

The Universe maintains a perfect balance among the things, creatures, and activities. So, just observe and allow the life to flow naturally. Live in the present, focusing on what you need to do right now and in the next moment. Avoid short cuts and act as per current observation. Say goodbye to procrastination and alternatives and do what is required. You will find that this way of working can lead to great achievements. Scientific breakthroughs often result from keen observations, and a deep understanding of natural world. Newton's apple serves as powerful reminder that by being present and attentive to the world around us we can unlock profound insight and make great discoveries.

Here is a small story to explain how mere observation can lead to big discoveries:

Once, in a soap manufacturing company a customer complaint surfaced. Retailers were finding empty soap covers within packed Cartons. The issue reached to the CEO through the quality manager and the CEO ordered the team to resolve it within a week. The team of engineers swung into action to find a solution.

A joint team of software and hardware engineers presented a solution. They suggested developing a sensor-based robotic arm fixed on the automatic packing conveyor. The sensor would detect empty soap cover, send signal to the robotic arm through software and the arm would pick up the empty cover, avoiding soap less cover entry into the final packed cartoon.

However, the CEO rejected this proposal expecting a more cost-effective solution.

Amidst this, a workman who diligently operated this assembly line day in and day out approached and said, "May I suggest something, sir?", "Your boss's idea has already been rejected; what do you want to suggest?" the CEO yelled. The operator replied, "Sir, we can install a large fan at the end of the packing conveyor. The blast of air will blow away the empty cover ensuring that only soap filled covers reach the packing carton". What a simple but effective observation!

The CEO was impressed by the simple solution and approved it immediately for implementation. He even announced an award for this observant operator. He asked this worker how he came up with such an intelligent solution. The operator humbly replied, " Sir, I spend hours observing the process during my shift and this simple solution naturally emerged.

This story is a testament to the power of observation. A simple act of keen observation can result in practical, cost effective and straight forward solutions to complex problems.

Our Psychology prevents us to observe

Let us understand it this way. Our mind keeps on running different movies for us. It is like a movie theater with three kinds of projectors.

The first projector replays movies from the past, featuring memories, traumas and pain. It projects scenes from your personal history.

The second projector projects a film from future, showcasing your goals ambitions; desires and fears. These scenes are hopes and worries about what is yet to come.

The third projector runs a film of present moments. Every moment of the day, it captures ongoing narratives, judgments, comments and worries your ego constructs about your present experience.

Throughout the day our ego keeps on watching these three movies. It watches a movie from the past, a daydream about the future, and if neither is happening, it narrates, judges, comments and worries about the present.

When we go to watch a movie in the theater, if the movie is engaging and the actors are talented, it captures us. We feel the joy and pain of the actor in the movie. We lose ourselves to the movie and feel the story as if it is our own.

Now imagine the movie playing in your mind. What if the actor or actress looks exactly like you and has the same name and is playing the same experience you are having? How could you not lose yourself in that movie? When we lose ourselves to the inner movie, we miss the present moment and close our minds and heart to the universe.

So, what can we do to prevent losing ourselves to this movie:

A) Create space and distance: Practice creating mental space and distance from movies plying in your mind. Step back and observe them as if you were an audience member rather than the main character.

B) Keep our minds and heart open: Stay receptive to the world around you. Cultivate an openness to new experiences rather than being solely engrossed in your inner movies.

C) Become a non-judgmental observer: Instead of constantly judging people and situations simply allow moments to unfold without imposing immediate judgments or preconceived notions.

Observe life in the present

Your life will be transformed if you start observing things simply as they unfold, instead of looking at them with prejudices. The catalyst for a great change is non-other than the present moment. Live each moment and don't waste life overthinking about the past or future. Observe every moment with full attention and take actions that are required to be taken at that moment. Somebody has rightly mentioned "where attention starts going; energy starts flowing."

If we start observing present moments, we can make our life very simple and joyful. The past resembles a bounced cheque with no value in the present context. And the future is like a Postdated cheque - You never know when it might get bounced. The present however is akin to hard cash in hand- a precious gift. Use it carefully.

Accept life as it comes to you. Keeping your attention firmly rooted in the present. In turn, this cosmos will take care of your future perfectly. With your attention in the present, you will require very less energy and effort to get things done. Which means you start becoming more productive and efficient.

The future is like a budding flower which will flourish naturally when nourished by the actions you take in the present. We must convince ourselves to understand that we can only work with what is on our hands right now and not with what is on our minds. This is the secret to live a fulfilling life and making the most of each precious moment.

Realization by observation

Life is a journey; enjoy it. Had it been a race, whoever finished first would've been the winner, but it is not like that, is it? We all want to live longer, and not finish our lives off before others.

Louis Agassiz, the great scientist, was very popular amongst his pupils. One day Louis entered the room with a flask of water with a fish swimming in it. He called one of the undergraduate students, who wanted to pursue his PHD under him and said, "Your job is to observe this fish without hurting it till you know everything about it." After saying this, Louis went away. The student, as per instructions, watched the fish for 2-3 hours, noted his observations. He went out to find Louis for sharing his observations but could not find his professor. He thought that he would explain his observation the next day to Louis. To his surprise, Louis disappeared from the place without telling anybody.

Now the student understood that his professor wanted him to devote more time observing and understanding the fish.

So, he studied it for an entire week. During this time, he made remarkable observations. Details that had previously gone unnoticed, such as the fish's teeth—each one varying in size—became strikingly clear now. He also noticed a surprising symmetry between the front and back, as well as the top and bottom parts of the body of the fish, all of which were now clearly visible. So, at the end of his observant week he explained his findings to Louis. But to his surprise Louis said these details were not enough. The student was quite determined and he wanted to do his research under this able guide only.

He decided to discard his old notes and embarked on the fresh round of observations dedicating another 70-80 hours to the task. This time he got surprised to see the detailing in the fish. He observed the fish's ability to change the color of skin throughout the day. He also identified special strips that allowed him to classify it into a distinct category of species. One particularly fascinating finding was that a change in temperature prompted the fish to change the direction in which it rotated it eyes.

When Professor Louis observed this student's notes, he declared, "Now you are ready to start the research work under my guidance".

Observation holds utmost importance not only in scientific observations but also in life itself. When we approach life with a mindful and observant attitude, paying full attention to the events and situations as they unfold— and respond thoughtfully rather than reacting impulsively we navigate our life's journey in the right direction.

It's natural to contemplate a situation, consider various possibilities and plan for different outcomes. However, excessive rumination dwelling on "what if's" and questioning your own abilities can lead to self-doubt. This Universe doesn't operate on your thinking or wishes. It operates on its own principles. Therefore, it's crucial to maintain focus on the present, being keenly observant and taking action. Remaining indecisive for a long time is also dangerous. It keeps on weakening you. Make decisions and move. You may take a wrong decision, but it'll give you fantastic learnings. So don't overthink; observe with focus and make a decision.

This life is a game and we all are the players. He who has good observation becomes a better player. He who observes more and practices more keeps refining his game and attains excellence.

DO IT YOURSELF

1. Take a moment to observe a flower attentively. How would you describe the emotions and feelings it evokes within you?

2. Reflect on your own focus and attentiveness while actively listening to others

3. Can you try undertaking two tasks with unwavering focus, without worrying about the outcome? Later reflect on the experience and share your thoughts with yourself.

4. How would you impart the principles of focused approach to your child?

5. Observe your child / younger brother-sister closely and identify valuable lessons or insights you can learn from their behavior and perspective.

INTELLECT & INTELLIGENCE

Synergy in cognition

"I know that I am intelligent because I know that I know nothing."

-Socrates

Human Intellect is undoubtedly a precious asset. But its value lies in how it is used. A sharp intellect is generally celebrated but it's crucial to realize that having a highly developed intellect, without a connection to universal wisdom can lead to its own set of challenges. Intellect is like a having a sharp knife, if not handled with care, it can harm the inner self. Unfortunately, the poor inner self lacks inherent defenses to protect itself against the misuse of intellect. We in the modern society emphasize a lot on the human beings. We celebrate our intellect over other creatures. The process of glorifying our ability to think works through the process of identification where we identify ourselves with various labels: name, religion, caste, nationality and what not. These identifications are built upon the impressions in our brains along with the data collected and stored by our six senses. The input for Intellect comes from these six senses, with which we try to understand the outer world. This process is essential for our survival as it helps us navigate and understand the external world.

Do you know what applying Intellect means?

It entails the process of processing the data stored in memory since birth. Based on that limited data in one's storage, which is accumulated through leanings, experiences, teachings, etc., collected through six senses, an individual tries to make decisions. The decisions we take today decide the next part of life. They contribute to develop our attitudes and expand our horizons.

Our senses give us comparative information. When it is dark, you understand light. When it is cold, you know heat. These sensory perceptions are relative and context dependent. Your dark might be light for other creatures. For instance, an owl may perceive light when a human might experience darkness. Our senses thus give us comparative information necessary for survival. But this information may be a distortion of reality. This recognition raises a question of whether there exists a reality beyond the scope of human intellect.

Indeed, a broader intelligence exists that extends beyond our external world. This universal intelligence revolves around the process of turning inward. Which we'll explore as we continue reading.

Essential nature of Human Intellect

The essential nature of human intellect often involves learning through dissection. Scientists commonly employ dissection as a method to understand various aspects of the world. For instance, doctors dissect frogs and mice to gain inside into their biological process and their life functions. Dissection provides valuable information but it is not sufficient for the comprehensive understanding of life.

Consider for instance the act of dissecting a flower. Through this process one can get knowledge about its construction and fragrance. However, it's important to note that once a flower is dissected, it can never be reassembled and the fragrance it once possessed vanishes. Natural intelligence on the other hand keeps it blooming for the whole of its life span.

We suffer our Intellect.

Our Intellect is a potent tool comparable to a sharp knife. Just as holding a sharp knife wrongly, can lead to self-inflicted harm, many individuals often misuse their Intellect, which results in self-inflicted emotional pain and dissatisfaction. It's a source of surprise when people wonder why they experience so much dissatisfaction.

The issue arises from the fact that we are using this tool without any user manual. Without proper guidance we become unwitting victims of our Intellect. The key lies in the learning how to use our intellect effectively and in the right direction. The sooner we realize this and embark on the path of understanding and mastering our intellect, the greater benefits we can reap.

Intellect losing importance

In this age of cutting-edge technology, scientists and technologists are developing artificial intelligence and machine learning. With this technology, the significance of human Intellect may diminish. Many of the secrets it once held are no longer as relevant. It's likely that numerous professions that exist today will become obsolete in next 15-20 years. Machine equipped with vast data and analytical capability will increasingly take over tasks that have traditionally relied on human intellect.

In this evolving landscape, it is possible that intellect itself will be commoditized and available in the market. Machine will do most of those activities for practically nothing that a person previously engaged in using their intellect. It's not farfetched to envision a future where "Robo Friends" will be available in the market. These robotic partners will be intellectually programmed to match individuals' habits and nature. They would interact with their human partner based on their emotions and be equipped to provide care and support - tailored to your needs.

As a result, humans will need to prove wisdom by engaging in the endeavors that extend beyond mere intellect, seeking to bring deeper meaning to their life, recognizing that their existence is relatively brief in the broader context of the universe

Limitation of Intellect and Life

Human Intellect does indeed have its limitations. Our thoughts are the product of our Intellect and they often lead us to believe that we are the owner of materialistic things including our physical bodies. It instills in us the sense of ownership over things like house, car, and even our relationships. As we become increasingly identified with these materialistic aspects of life, our mind wants to protect them. In the process of protection, it builds mental walls for safety. Over the time these mental walls can start to feel constricting and the cycle continues as the mind erects even more significant limits. This ongoing imprisonment persists because fundamentally, humans possess a nature inclined towards liberation. However, the intellect often keeps us away from achieving that liberation.

Individually we are mere micro specks in front of the mighty universe. Yet we possess a substantial ego that inflates our importance. Just think how many big shorts have come and gone in this materialist world before your appearance. Where are they today? All of them are part of the topsoil. Isn't it? It's a sobering reminder that we all share the same fate ultimately. Everyone has an expiry date. But under the influence of our Intellect, we act as if we will remain here forever.

If we remember our death without fear, we will realize how short this life is! It can inspire us to lead a more meaningful existence guided by the deeper connection to universal intelligence which can lead to a sense of liberalization and fulfillment.

Universal Intelligence

There exists a form of natural intelligence that underlies the very existence of the universe. It is this intelligence that ensures planets, Stars, and millions of galaxies coexist for millions of years without colliding. Every day we see the sun shine without fail. A million functions of our bodies continue to operate even when our conscious mind has gone to sleep. We still breathe in sleep and our blood constantly circulates to every cell, without any conscious effort or thought. This implies the presence of an intelligence that transcends human intellect and functions beyond our awareness.

This intelligence operates beyond the limits of human understanding and is capable of manifesting inner wonders. It remains pure and untouched by limitation of human memory. To tap into this profound experience, we must refrain from identifying ourselves with external constructs. As we do so we can access extraordinary powers and natural capabilities.

The more we grow the inner connection, the closer we come to the inner peace and self-alignment. Understanding and harnessing pure intelligence has the potential to elevate human experiences to unprecedented levels. Opportunities become boundless and with nurturing the inner experience of intelligence, we can perform our jobs with significantly less effort. Our overall effectiveness goes to the next level beyond the expectation of this world, leading to sense of delight and fulfillment within ourselves.

Human Creation and Universal Creation

Let us remember where we originally came from. A long time ago, our true home was the absolute reality of the spiritual divine order and intelligence. Over time, humans deviated from this spiritual realm slowly and started developing their relative existence in this material world. This transformation unfolded slowly, driven by the actions that contradicted the law of nature often fueled by selfishness and egocentrism. By doing so, we did something new that did not exist. We started creating things like illness, hunger, fear, etc.

When we faced these kinds of issues, our ego started using intellect to find temporary solutions to these problems. Intellect is our marvelous tool to solve problems by finding solutions to safeguard our ego and its identification with our physical bodies.

So, with our Intellect, we formulated various solutions. For example, for illness, we developed drugs, radiation, surgical procedure. In response to hunger, we developed fertilizers, pesticides, irrigation techniques etc. To address fear, our Intellect led us to create weapons for protection, surveillance systems and advanced technology. However, the interesting fact is that none of these solutions succeeded in eradicating illness, hunger or fear.

On the other hand, universal intelligence possesses an abundance that knows no bounds. It transcends limitations. Free from fear, memory and constrain of time. When our Chitta is synchronized /connected with universal intelligence, we overcome all factors like fear, hunger, illness, ego, etc. This connection is also part of our inheritance and a divine order. Universal Intelligence encompasses all that is extraordinary and is within our power to attune ourselves to its frequency.

Getting prepared for universal linkage

One wonderful way to connect with the universal energies is to understand meditation and embracing meditative state.

Meditation: Meditation is a process or practice that involves nurturing mind. Through meditation, wisdom bosoms, enabling you to perceive things as they truly are. With consistent meditation practice, you gain mastery over your mind, gradually enhancing your ability to comprehend the realities of inner world.

Meditation is such an enriching and vast subject that many books can be written on this topic. Here I'll provide you an overview and offer some tips for meditation. There are different types of meditation techniques present in the spiritual world.

You might have encountered different names such as sound meditation which focuses on sound awareness. Transcendental meditation involving the repetition of Mantras and Visualization techniques as emphasized by institutions like Brahma Kumaris. Other methods include Anapana and Vipassana meditation.

You can choose any meditation technique that resonates with you. Few Indian meditation techniques like Samantha meditation and Vipasna meditation have been practiced over 2500 years and are attributed to Mahatma Buddha. Buddha after attaining enlightenment described these techniques as "Dhyana".

A) Samatha Meditation

B) Vipasana

Samatha Meditation:

Purpose: To cultivate calmness, serenity and peacefulness. It prepares you before you dive deep into your inner world.

Analogy: Imagine the mind as a lake. if the lake's water is not clean, is full of algae and ripples arise now and then, you will not be able to see the bottom of the lake from the top. After performing Samatha, you can see deep into your inner self during Vipassana. Samatha and Vipassana are interrelated and cannot be separated.

Practicing tips

1. Sit in Padma asana or some comfortable mode on the ground.
2. Keep your eyes open. Bring both eyeballs to focus on the center of the nose.
3. Keep your breath natural.
4. Try to focus on the nose. Your mind will get itself diverted. Bring it back and focus with open eyes towards the nose.

Practice it regularly, start with ten minutes daily

B) Vipassana Meditation: During Vipasana practitioners observe bodily sensation, thoughts, and emotions with deep mindfulness. Gautam Budha enlightened many with Vipasna at his time and since then, people in the spiritual world have been using this dhyana.

Purpose: It trains you to watch things as they are

Meaning: To see through something.

Practicing tips:

1) Sit in Padma asana or some comfortable mode keeping backbone straight

2) Focus on your breaths

3) Train yourselves to see things as they truly are

4) Gradually shift your attention to a body scan. Start from top of head and move down to toes, paying attention to each part of body.

5) Notice any sensation whether it is pleasant, unpleasant or neutral

6) Cultivate a sense of equanimity or mental calmness

7) Maintain continuous awareness of bodily sensation and breath

8) Observe feeling and thoughts without any judgment

9) Stay in present moment

10) Start the short sessions and gradually extend the duration

Vipasana is an effective technique and getting very popular throughout the world.

In India nowadays, Goyanka Ji is the founder of Vipasana institutes. He learned it from Berma and came back to India. Vipassana was adopted by jail authorities for their prisoners, hard-core criminals and the effects were quite satisfying. It was practiced in Jaipur Jail and Vadodara Jail for reformations. The most known case of Vipasna implementation is Tihar Jail of Delhi. Dr. Kiran Bedi, who was in-charge of the Tihar Jail, took this initiative and transformed the life of many prisoners during her tenure.

There are Vipassana centers in different cities of India. A training course of 10 days in Vipassana is very satisfying in all the centers. First three days, you perform the ANAPANA technique, where you focus on your breaths and reset for seven days; you focus on different parts of the body. During increasing focus on your various body parts, you have different blissful feelings associated with the process. After that, you practice activating your seven chakras.

Practicing Tips ANAPANA:

Sit in a relaxed posture. Keep your backbone and Neck straight and eyes closed. Remove accessories like specs, goggles, etc. Start focusing on your breaths. Slowly be very attentive and very focused on your breaths. Watch your incoming breath as well as going breath. Increase your focus. You become the watchman on the door of your nozzles. Not a single breath goes inside without your watch. Your mind may get distracted. Bring the mind back to your breaths. Keep watching your breaths.

You can start Annapana for 10 minutes daily to begin with. Then, choose your coach /master. Under his guidance, you can practice your meditation and be the master slowly.

DO IT YOURSELF

1. Reflect on your understanding of the nature of your Intellect. How does it influence your thoughts, decisions and overall perception of the world around you?

2. How can we align yourself with Universal Intelligence?

3. Explain to yourself the power of Universal intelligence.

4. On what basis does human Intellect work?

5. Experiment with tuning yourself to capture a specific frequency of universal intelligence.

STABLE INNER BASE

Serenity nexus

"Your mind knows only some things. Your inner voice, your instinct, knows everything. If you listen to what you know instinctively, it will always lead you down the right path."

- Henry Winkler

You cannot feel the exuberance of life without having a calm stable inner (mind). A creative explosion is only possible with stability. Imagine a personality that navigates through the heights of success without getting swept away and weathers the lows of failures without losing its balance. The primary requirement of being alive and lively is a stable inner base. So let your inner stable base be the magic that turns the ordinary into an extraordinary adventure!

Balance in Life

Like a bicyclist who has to stake balance while peddling, life demands our efforts to find equilibrium. If the cyclist doesn't know how to make balance, he'll fall. Similarly, a car driver needs to find equilibrium between the three pedals to avoid crashing. In our life we are the drivers and without an inner stable foundation we may encounter frequent accidents.

In the initial phase of martial arts training, instructors first teach you to master posture, of aligning yourself with gravity. Well, this is not just about physical form, but to build a strong foundation as no matter what techniques you learn, the stability of the legs and body will form the bedrock for all the moves. Just as a strong stance in martial arts is necessary to execute techniques with precision and power, a stable foundation in life enables one to navigate challenges and grow with purpose.

In this fast-paced life, most of us are racing ahead with technology, often without a stable base. Just imagine someone who is yet to learn coordinating between the three pedals of a car, but is speeding on a highway. The result would be disastrous, wouldn't it? You must have come across people who have succeeded but need help to sustain their success. This is because they were unprepared for the challenges that come with being at the pinnacle. The real challenge isn't succeeding, but in the sustenance of success.

The stress of (so-called) success

The pressure and stress associated with success can be stressful. In an attempt to cope up, some individuals turn to alcohol or drugs, seeking a temporary escape for their overwhelmed brain. It's ironic that, despite the remarkable development and capabilities of the human brain to get us out of any situation, there is a desire to quiet it momentarily for the sake of peace! This self-imposed struggle often comes from feeling that success has somehow taken the control.

Similarly, people facing successive failures, may plunge into deep sorrow, vowing never to try the same things for the rest of their lives due to fear embedded their minds.

Elders may offer advice to exercise self-control for stability. But stability doesn't mean trimming down on your energy and vitality. You cannot sacrifice vibrance, passion and the zest of life for the sake of attaining stability. Stability without the zeal of life is like the stability of a rock – lifeless and unalive. Balance that comes out of curtailment will never have desirable results. For genuine inner stability, clarity of vision is paramount. As explored in this chapter, our external and internal environment co exists. Therefore, it is crucial to dedicate few minutes daily to access and nurture internal environment for lasting stability.

Strengthen your foundation

In life there are moments when external events disturb and shake us to the core. Setbacks often make us distressed; some people try to normalize constantly being in a state of anxiety.

If we neglect our inner world, we may find ourselves in perpetual state of unease – so much so that distress starts feeling like a normal phenomenon.

At these times, we must reflect into our inner selves and convey a strong message to our subconscious-affirming a sturdy foundation. Declare "Nothing can shake my foundation; come what may."

I usually find my inner self disturbed when things don't unfold as expected. The truth is that my irritation is always a result of my own reaction to external circumstances. No one has the power to shake or irritate me without my permission. When someone speaks negatively about me in my presence, it starts igniting my inner fire, making me furious and eager to react. This very reaction becomes the catalyst for further internal disturbance, dragging me into a vicious cycle.

The key to maintaining inner stability lies in choosing not to react impulsively but to respond wisely. Mind it, when faced with a challenging situation, refrain from immediate reaction. Instead take a brief pause, allowing your inner self a few seconds to offer valuable guidance. Seek permission from within and respond responsibly.

"Between stimulus and yourself lies the power to respond." Viktor E Frankl

If you adopt this approach, nobody can make you annoyed or happy without your permission. Inner stability means not allowing others to dictate your emotions; you are the master of your mind. You won't utter, "He made me furious," recognizing that though he did his karma by speaking negatively about you, but it will be your choice of reacting or responding that will reflect your actions, and that will be completely in your power. This way you take control of yourself.

Only you can motivate yourself.

Motivation is an internal drive that only you can ignite within yourself. Also, you cannot control anyone and no one can control you. Parents for instance may wish to guide their children, wanting to control them. However, little ones resist control. If we cannot control our children who have been with us all their lives, how do we expect to control others-independent people with diverse backgrounds; in nature, culture, experience and religion? Even with the best intention, imposing our will upon others rarely leads to positive results.

In your family life avoid expecting too much from others, especially in parenting. Parenting is a challenging process. Remember, your children are not your possessions; you don't own them. While they have come through you and it is your responsibility to provide them with a free and healthy environment to grow. You must not project your own expectations on to them. You can only motivate people to change, but the key to any results is their willingness to be influenced and their will to change.

Incorporating yoga and meditation into your morning routine will motivate you make your inner self stable. Take time to observe your thoughts and strive to make them pure and positive each day. Reserve moments for internal reflection and be mindful of the mental content you consume.

The only stable is Vibrant.

In the Indian mythology lord Shiva is associated with stability. Shiva also represents dance. As mentioned earlier, inner dance and ecstasy are not possible without stability.

It is unfortunate that a significant portion of humanity, even in adulthood, is emotionally immature. Let us explore this through various unstable behaviors in our society. Many of us while driving a car engage in criticizing and abusing other drivers on the road. If someone is moving slower than us, they are labeled an idiot, and if someone is going faster, they become a maniac. If stuck in traffic for a minute, we often turn to checking our cell phones. Some one of us become disturbed if our social media post doesn't receive sufficient likes, we start doubting and questioning why others' content is going viral and not ours. Someone travelling a road might consistently focus on and criticize potholes, blaming the corporation or the government regularly. It looks like potholes from the road have found a place in one's mind. All these behaviors stem from nervous energy and an unstable inner environment that consistently leads to a feeling of unhappiness or disturbance.

The frequency of negative emotions such as anxiety, depressive thoughts, bad memories, sadness, guilt fears, phobias, and resentment can significantly impact our wellbeing and make us shaky. These emotions, if left unaddressed tend to act as limiting factors, gradually eroding our resilience and vitality. Similar to termites that silently hollow the core of structure, these emotions can hollow us out from within.

Behavioral patterns like laziness, procrastination, lack of motivation, etc. keep on degrading us day by day. Recognizing and addressing these factors by mindful thinking will help gaining stability.

Be aware of your thoughts.

It is our responsibility to manage our emotions. Remaining aware of them, we need to train ourselves to consciously choose positive emotions while avoiding those that limit us. Failing to take charge of this responsibility can turn our own intellect against us.

When faced with a situation different from our desires, our minds tend to think in many directions often leading to a state of confusion. During such situations the mind starts painting negative pictures, creating a series of causes and effects. It's like being a balloon in the air whose path is defined not by itself, but by external winds. But if we are aware of our thought, we can realize that most of our fears are not based on reality. Instead, we fabricate them when circumstances are not in our favor. This self-generated fear pushes many of us to give up.

Be stable and never quit.

How we respond, not react, determines whether we have good or bad day. It's a choice which we must make every day to remain positive. Although time is ticking away, life doesn't run faster than a day at a time. Each day is a new opportunity. And there is always time to start afresh, with a stable base. Don't hesitate to take initiative, regardless of the stage of life you find yourself in. KFC was started by Colonel Sanders after his retirement! Abraham Lincoln reached the pinnacle of his career much later than anyone would've expected.

So, wake up each morning with new energy, thanking the supreme power for the new day- the new chance to do better. Remember, you won't regret the failures in you life as much as you'd regret the beginnings that never took place. Whatever you think is right for you, just do it. Don't postpone things indefinitely. Let us learn to choose our emotions and realize that the source of peace lies within.

Mind It - A stable mind is your best friend in adversity.

DO IT YOURSELF

1. Recall on a time when you remained stable in a difficult situation and describe the experience of enhanced effectiveness within yourself.

2. Try choosing happiness in a difficult situation. Share the impact, recognizing that it doesn't necessarily negate the challenge but avoids unnecessary stress.

3. Initiate the practice of Yoga Asanas under someone's guidance.

4. Incorporate a routine of sitting calmly for a few moments without any thought.

OUR PSYCHOLOGY

&

THE FACTUAL REALITY

Beyond perception

"Look up at the stars and not down at your feet. Try to make sense of what you see, and wonder about what makes the universe exist. Be curious."

-Stephen Hawking

Once there was a person who devotedly worshipped God. One day, God appears and offers to grant him any wish. The man jumps with joy, but God puts a unique condition: whatever he receives his neighbor would get double.

Upon hearing this, all his happiness vanishes. He wonders whether God is really fulfilling his desires or subjecting him to torment. Seeking guidance, the man asks God for permission to consult his Lawyer before making any decision. So, he approaches his lawyer. And explains to him that he was happy with what he would receive but he couldn't understand why the neighbor should get something better.

The wise lawyer advices him to first test whether God is really ready to bless him with whatever he wants. He suggests the man to first demand a five-story house as trial. The man goes to God and asks for a five-story house for himself. To his surprise, in no time he finds himself in a lavish building, but he looks outside and finds that the neighbor's houses are converted into ten-story buildings.

So he goes to his lawyer to complains that the neighbors got houses better than his. The lawyer comes up with a plan and suggests him to ask for a deep well in front of this five story house. The man asks God and a deep well appears in front of the house. Consequently, the neighbors get two wells in front of their houses and the man remains unhappy.

The lawyer says, "Don't worry, now ask God to blow off one of your eyes." The man asked the same to God and in a moment, he became Boss-eyed. Now each of his neighbors loses two eyes and becomes blind.

God asks, "Are you happy now?" The man replies, "Yes, I am, a little. But I'll be happier once these blind neighbors tumble off their tall buildings into the wells dug in front of their houses." God said, "But you lost your eye. He said "it's alright because sometimes sacrifices are necessary to attain something better!"

People find more joy seeing others suffer than in celebrating their own success!

Everybody believes that they are more deserving than others and strive to appear superior. Our education systems teach us the idea of being ahead of others in class. People are in a rat race to claim the top spot. This is a meaningless race. The concept of competition can sometimes foster a mindset where individuals want to perceive others as struggling or performing poorly. It's as if they take pleasure in the misfortunes or weaknesses of others to elevate themselves.

People often engage in comparing while evaluating their health, wealth and possessions. They spend a whole lifetime comparing themselves to others. However, it doesn't take long for all these achievements to the root cause of the mental disturbance rather than peace. The feeling of emptiness prevails in a much stronger way. In the phase of this significant loss, the question that arises is how to live differently, joyfully and blissfully without the unnecessary drama? Life is too precious to be dedicated solely to earning a livelihood or accumulating material wealth.

Psychological drama has nothing to do with reality:

The emotional narratives which we create for ourselves are often filled with anxiety and negative thoughts, are not necessarily reflective of objective reality. The stories we tell in our mind might not always match what's really happening. Our psychological dramas are often exaggerated, distorted and based on perception rather than factual reality.

Our psychology is a drama that is poorly directed by us. And by giving it better direction we can tap into natural intelligence. The sooner we realize the facts of life and become self-aware, the better we can live our life.

We don't see things as they are. We see things as we are:

In Pittsburg on 19th April 1999, a robber named McArthur robbed two banks in a single day. He not only robbed banks with complete confidence without wearing any mask but also smiled at the cameras during the robbery. Police caught hold of him within a day with the help of surveillance camera footage. Interestingly when he was handcuffed, he expressed confusion mumbling, "but I wore the juice." This statement left everyone puzzled

On questioning, he told the Police that he was surprised at how his face was revealed to the cameras, because he had applied lemon juice to his face! He believed that applying lemon juice makes a face invisible as it was known that lemon juice was used to make invisible ink. The police, listening to his baseless story, tested him for mental issues, but it turned out he was neither mentally ill, nor under the influence of any drugs.

This funny robbery incident inspired social psychologists Dunning and Kruger to delve deeper into this phenomenon. Specifically, the robber's confidence attracted their attention leading them to conduct some experiments on a group of students.

They conducted tests on Grammar, logical reasoning and sense of humor for the students. After completing test, students were instructed to evaluate themselves based on the test and give themselves marks on their performance.

Upon analyzing their actual performance to their perceived marks, Dunning and Kruger found that the poor performers gave themselves high marks while those who actually achieved very high marks evaluated themselves relatively lower.

Denning and Kruger then extended their experiments on another set of people including drivers in America and professors of universities. They found that 80% of drivers in America thought that their driving skills were above average.

Finally, Denning and Kruger proved their hypothesis that people with less knowledge and skill are often confident of possessing good knowledge. Whereas those with good knowledge and skill think that others are equally or more knowledgeable, leading them to undervalue themselves. This concept is known as the Denning and Kruger effect in psychology.

In our everyday experience, we usually come across individuals who, despite having little knowledge, confidently boast about their expertise. This is not uncommon in the corporate world, where certain managers, posing as leaders exhibit unwarranted confidence without possessing required skill and knowledge. Unfortunately, these people ruin the organization in long term. On the flipside there are those who possess substantial expertise but consistently underestimate themselves and never come up the corporate ladder.

Denning and Kruger effect is a cognitive bias with which we all suffer at some point in time. It involves a gap between perceived ability and actual ability is typically blind to the individual concerned.

After reading some article or a book or having little experience in a subject, we might feel over confident thinking we understand it well. But with time, when we gain knowledge and real experience, we realize that we were initially far from the truth. Sometimes we are unaware of our own ignorance

On the flip side, when we possess knowledge about a subject, we might assume others understand it at the same level. This can lead to frustration when others do not grasp what seems simple to us.

Denning and Kruger effect can be explained by the following figure:

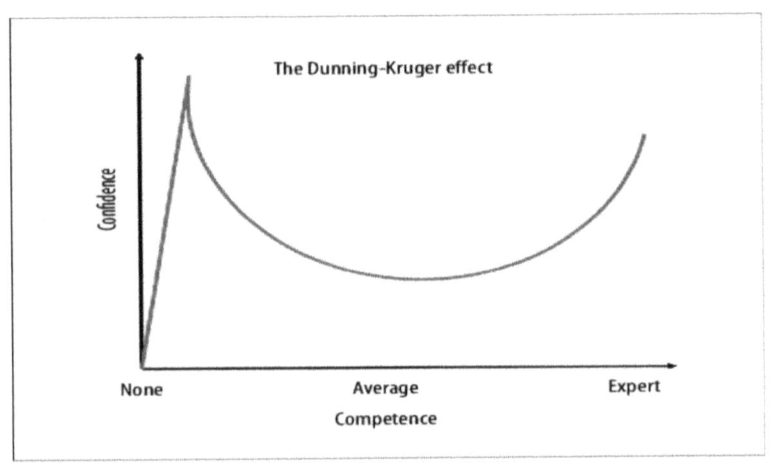

The X- axis represents the competence and the Y- axis represents confidence. Initially, when one has little knowledge, his confidence level is sky-high. When you start gaining knowledge, confidence takes a sharp decline. You start knowing that there is a lot to learn and you're just scratching the surface.

At a certain point the need for both knowledge and confidence arise. However continuous learning leads to an eventual improvement in confidence. With further learning, the confidence increases aligning with a more accurate and justified level of confidence based on genuine knowledge.

"The more you know, the more you know you do not know" **Aristotle**

"I do not know, and I don't care, and it doesn't make any difference" **Albert Einstein**

Once we know this concept of active bias, we should doubt our very high confidence and focus on gaining skill and knowledge.

While I don't claim expertise in phycology, I offer insides drawn from my personal journey and encounters with various concepts. My experiences although limited, fuel my commitment to continually enhance my understanding in the subject. The intention is to share thoughts that resonate with an eagerness to learn and grow.

One such concept I came across in my early professional life is Johari's Window Model developed by famous psychologists Joseph Luft and Harrington Ingham in 1955.

This simple yet powerful tool is designed to enhance self-awareness, high self-esteem and better interpersonal skill development.

It operates by assisting individuals visualize the variance between their self-perception and how others perceive them. This tool helps individuals to understand their thoughts on who they think they are and to get feedback from others on how they are perceived.

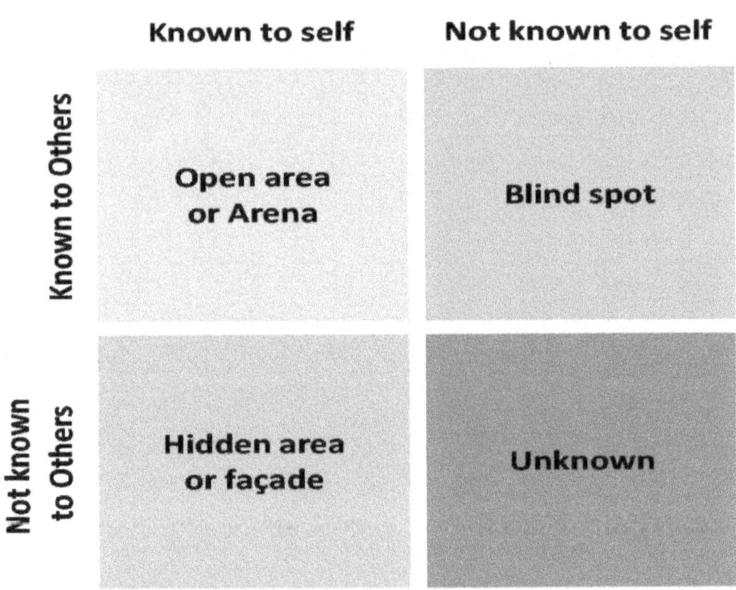

The Johari Window Model

As it's clear from the figure the four quadrants of the window are as following:

Open Area/Arena: - Aspects known by both self and others

Certain things about yourself are known to you as well as others, like your height, color, name, etc. This is the window where I am aware of that I know and others are also familiar with these aspects about me.

Blind spot: - In this window I am unaware of certain aspects about me that other know. This window tells me that I don't know that don't know, but others know about me.

Hidden Area/Facade: - Aspects known to self but unknown to others.

This is the window tells me that there are aspects which only I know and others don't know about me

Unknown: - Aspects unknown to both self or others i.e. I don't know and others also don't know.

We need to reduce the Blind window through open and sincere discussion about ourselves. Seek feedback from others and take corrective measures when required.

Self-awareness and attitude of learning:

Once we are aware and self-conscious, we adopt a learning attitude. As Jeff Keller said, "Attitude is the window through which we see things. Filthy things keep accumulating on this window over time. It needs to be cleaned from time to time. Everyone is born with a clean window." As you grow up, it is up to you, how much you let other people's influence tarnish that window. Attitude plays a vital role in our success. In corporate world, individuals at top of the pyramid rely 90% attitude and 10% skills. Conversely those at bottom side of pyramid use 90% skills and 10% attitude.

According to Dr. Vivek Bindra, "Attitude is based on seed patterns and flow of desires". It is up to us which kind of seeds we cultivate.

Let us be aware of our patterns. Keep learning to change our negative patterns. Be creative; let us create new opinions, explore new choices and strive to become better.

DO IT YOURSELF

1. Reflect on a past real-life situation where your fear led to indecision only to discover that reality turn out differently.

2. Evaluate your level of concerns for others' opinion. If it's significant. Consider how can you reorganize yourself to lessen its impact.

3. Take stock of your efforts to clean your window through which you see the world.

4. Cultivate the habit of getting feedback about yourself as a means of self-improvement.

HORIZON OF GRATITUDE
The grateful infinity

"A grateful mind is a great mind which eventually attracts to itself great things."
-Plato

"I don't have to chase extraordinary moments to find happiness - it's right in front of me if I'm paying attention and practicing gratitude."

-Brene Brown

I strongly believe in the Law of attraction. Expressing gratitude enhances relationships and draws the right people into your life. Gratitude can eradicate negativity; it's indeed great blessing for us.

The secret of gratitude:

Here is a secret about appreciation. When you convey thanks and exhibit selflessness, nature responds by granting you more happiness. Nature is bound to give you back. It becomes a reciprocal exchange. Once we are grateful, we appreciate the goodness of life. Reflect on how you can deepen the sense of gratitude. The more we cultivate thankfulness, the happier we become.

Once, a man reaches heaven after his death. There he embarks on a tour. He notices a massive room with many angels working on different files. Curiously he asks, "What are you all doing? Why does everyone seem so busy?" One angel responds, "This is our incoming section. Whenever someone on earth expresses desire, we attach their willingness to their file."

After listening to this, the man moves to the next room. It is a comparatively tiny room with very few angels working there. He asks, "What is the purpose of this room." The angels reply, "This is our outgoing section. We cannot fulfill every desire as someone prays for rain while another wants the sun to shine. So, we are very selective about fulfilling desires based on various factors."

Continuing the tour, he enters even a smaller room with only one person working there. He inquires, "Why is there only one angel here and almost no work load?" "This is our acknowledgment section." Replied the angel "It is rare for the people to send an acknowledgment after their desires have been fulfilled."

Frequently we overlook acknowledging our blessings. Our actions reflect a relentless pursuit of desires. We pray for things thinking they are most important, but once we get them, we want something else. It feels like a never-ending cycle. We are always so busy running after desires that we forget to appreciate what we already have. In this race of fulfilling desires, we have no sense of fulfillment. We will always feel burdened by desires unless we become grateful for everything we are already blessed with.

It all begins in childhood. A child with lots of toys gets tired of them and runs to grab other child's toys. We eat good food at home every day, we always desire to go to a restaurant to eat different food. Its only when we are far from home do we realize the importance of homemade food. Someone with a bicycle desires a motorbike. One who possesses a motorbike wants a car. The car owner may prefer a more luxurious car or a helicopter. This desire continues, leading to frustration. We must break this cycle and appreciate what we have. This doesn't mean that we should not aim for a better life, but this Law of gratitude teaches that being grateful attracts more to be thankful for.

The culture of Gratitude starts from family:

Lack of gratitude is a blessing blocker. When a child takes their parent's efforts for granted, viewing their actions as mere duties, without appreciating the sacrifices they've made, it reflects ingratitude.

One of the biggest disappointments for a parent is when their child shows no sign of gratitude for all they have done for him/her. A mother wakes up early in the morning to cook lunch for her child's school, but the child not only neglects to say thank you but also refuses to eat it.

Parents make financial sacrifices, foregoing their desires to afford hobby class for their child. However, the child accuses them of not caring simply saying, "You don't care for me." Even when a father buys a smartphone for the child, and asks to limit its use during exams for the child's own benefit, a heated argument begins. The child not only fails to acknowledge the parent's effort but also communicates disrespectfully.

Parents dedicate a full day for their children - Cooking, cleaning, dropping them off at school, picking them up, and taking them for shopping- doing everything for them. However, when asked to do one thing for the parent, the response is a flat refusal. This constant struggle raises a question: Why should parents fight with their children every time they need something done? The child becomes affectionate and talkative when in need, saying, "Papa this! Mommy that!" when the child needs something, he becomes all starry-eyed. But, after the need is fulfilled, no longer pays attention to the parents, viewing them as annoying. Is the father merely viewed as the family's financial engine? As parents grapple with this challenging dynamic, what proactive steps can they take to navigate and address the challenges at hand?

They'll sulk. They'll fight. They try to ignore it. They don't know what to do.

One obvious solution could be, "why not tell a child everything you do for them? But many parents think, "Why should we have to say it? Can't they see it themselves? Only if we ask, and then they do something nice, then it's of no value. We don't want to beg for their attention and care. They should do it themselves." Ok, you won't ask; they are not doing it independently. What's the solution, then? Keep getting disappointed and give up?

Here is something important to consider: Gratitude is the super important thing for our interpersonal well-being. For your own happiness, your child's well-being, and the success of your relationships, cultivating gratitude is essential. You teach your children basic things like using the bathroom, language, and you teach them how to count: it's just as important to teach them how to be grateful to people as well.

It's really unfortunate that not everyone realizes how big of a deal gratitude is. We hope that children will develop gratitude on their own, but actively teaching them this important trait is crucial. First things first, learn to be grateful yourself. If you can't, don't try to teach children. Talk about how grateful you are to your parents, even when you've had conflicts in your home.

Interpersonal gratitude is partially dependent on empathy. Unless children know the costs you are paying to bring them up, unless they can look at your difficulties from your perspective, they won't truly get how much you are doing for them. So, you have to tell them very explicitly. If you woke up too early for them and felt tired the whole day, or if you are suppressing your desires to save money for them, talk about it. Don't just talk about what you are doing but also about what you are going through inside. This is not about showing off; it's about helping them see things they might not notice.

But caution:

a) Don't act like you are doing them a huge favor by having them and raising them. That attitude is not wise. Even though everything you are doing for them, you started a family because it fulfilled something for you. When you teach them gratitude, it has to go both ways. You too find satisfaction of being a parent through them.

b) Once they understand the efforts you are making for them, they will automatically show empathy with your struggles. This understanding becomes the foundation of their thankfulness

Gratitude is a choice:

Once, a news reporter visited a village suffering with drought. Curious about the impact on villagers he approached and asked a farmer about his life. The farmer expressed the sense of hardship, stating," My soil becomes hard, my cow is becoming older and weaker, and my health is not good. Life seems to be growing more cursed with each passing day."

Undeterred, the reporter sought another perspective from a different former in the village. This former chose gratitude. Saying, "Yes, the soil of my field is hard too, but I remember the time when I had no field at all. Today, at least, I have my own field, and with the help of my fellow villagers, we work hard to plough and can grow our seasonal crops". He continued, "My cow is aging, but it is still giving me milk. My family and I have enough milk to drink and even sell some for income. Even though I'm getting older, my health is better than many others."

This sentiment of gratitude should be reflected in every situation of life. Again, it's our choice. We can either spend our life lamenting the things we lack or be grateful for both the tangible and intangible things we already have. The power to decide rests with us.

Practicing Gratitude:

Nurture a conscious effort to appreciate small things in life. Each morning express gratitude for waking up, for the refreshing moments of your bath, and for the nourishment provided by your breakfast.

As you nourish gratitude for these simple things, more fulfilling picture of life will unfold. You will discover an increasing sense of contentment. Gratefulness has the transformative ability to lift your life to new heights inviting blessings from the universe. By expressing thanks for everything, you create a positive cycle where you receive even more gratitude, contributing to your overall happiness.

Gratitude serves as a powerful shift from self-pity to joy. To truly experience the benefits of gratitude, let the feeling resonate in your emotions. Be genuinely thankful for everything. Once gratitude becomes a part of you extend this positive energy beyond yourself to those in your surroundings.

Numerous research studies have proven that when you practicing gratitude can improve the brain plasticity. It establishes neural pathways and activates highly evolved areas of the brain. Over time your deep belief system sinks into your subconscious mind leading to a profound sense of fulfillment. As this impression takes roots in your *Chita*, you gain the power to manifest positive changes. It forms the foundation of personal growth.

Practice it for everything:

I am grateful that I am alive today.

I am grateful for my past accomplishments.

I am thankful for my focus on the present moment.

I wish to thank my parents, teachers and friends.

I am thankful to my family.

I am grateful for the challenges I faced.

I am thankful for the lessons I have learned.

I am grateful for all my highs and lows.

I am thankful for the skill and knowledge I achieved.

I am grateful for the progress I am making.

I am grateful for all of my blessings.

I am thankful; for the journey called life.

I am grateful for my uniqueness of mine.

I am grateful to the vision and passion I possess.

I am grateful for the present moment I am in.

I am thankful for the food I eat.

I am grateful for to help I received.

I am great full to my feelings and emotions.

I am thankful to my conscious and subconscious mind.

I am grateful for the energy I have.

I am thankful to the society I live in.

I am grateful for the desire to know myself.

I am thankful for my efforts in the improvement.

DO IT YOURSELF

1. Name three things for which you are grateful today. How do they impact your life and relationship?

2. Connect with nature, how does it make you feel grateful?

3. Can you think of a situation where expressing gratitude improved your relationship?

4. Observe yourself - How consistent are in expressing gratitude?

SELF DEVELOPMENT

&

SOCIAL RESPONSIBILITY

*Growing within and
giving back*

*"Through selfless service, you will always
be fruitful and find the fulfillment of
your desires,"*

-Bhagwat Geeta.

Acquiring knowledge and believing in something is one thing, but experiencing it strengthens conviction. Sharing these experiences with the society fosters human evolution. Our knowledge and experiences should extend beyond our lifetime, reaching as many people as possible to positively influence the society.

People don't care how much you know, but they know how much you care!

Instilling the idea of selfless service should be imbibed in youth from a young age, both at home as well as in schools. It is vital for addressing the challenge of helping the needy. Unfortunately, most modern educational institutions focus on preparing students for jobs, overlooking real life lessons.

Schools overlook that there is more to life than just survival. If our schools and society start teaching life's basics, guiding students to explore their inner selves, we will be able to build a much better society.

Once you pursue your passion, money and resources will naturally follow, providing you with more than what your initially require. This in turn enables you to make meaningful contribution to the society in many ways.

Today, many youngsters aren't keen on deviling into the life's philosophy. They often view this phase of life as one meant for enjoyment rather than embracing what seems like boring life lessons. They feel these lessons are for the grownups, yet the truth is the earlier you learn, the more you benefit.

Wholeheartedly adopting life's principles isn't a personal choice; it's a responsibility. This commitment urges us to actively share knowledge and happiness with others. We should start walking the talk. Individually we must make it our mission to imbibe the correct principles of life into the society. Those who have grown themselves successfully in different inner dimensions consistently promote message of peace and happiness.

Before exploring the topics of self and social responsibility, let us learn about commitment.

A middle- aged man having a heavy bag on his back was climbing a hill alongside many devotees to reach a temple on the hilltop. During his rest break, he saw a 15-year-old girl carrying her brother on her back, entirely devoted to reach the temple. Surprised with her energy he asked the girl if she was not tired. The girl looking at the man, replied, "You are tired because you have weight on your back, but I'm not as I have my brother on my shoulders and he is my responsibility."

Responsibility is never granted; it is always taken. When pursuing for your life goals, be ready for the consequences. Your desire comes with strings attached. Once we understand the responsibility towards ourselves, we'll become responsible for the society. There is no need to overwhelm ourselves with extra social responsibilities. Your responsible behavior automatically makes you accountable to the community.

Flowers in flowerpots arranged on a stage for visiting delegates don't have any extra responsibility to make them happy. A fully blossomed flower is nature's beauty and it just blooms, automatically bringing joy to many when arranged on stage. Becoming socially responsible needs an essential trait of being self-responsible.

Similarly, the sun is present in its place without any intent to give heat or light and without any expectation to get something back. We know very well that life on Earth is possible because of sun exists. Trees don't think about how much oxygen they've contributed; Its only us who are often in a mindset of possession and doer ship (refer to chapter number two). I passed exam, I showed him the right path. I did charity etc.-always occupied with self -

gratifying. We need to use our wisdom to shift from this "me" world to a "we" world by being ready for selfless giving.

In today's world, people have made social responsibility a means to display and assert superiority over others. However, this mere show-off doesn't truly make us socially responsible. In the corporate sector, many CSR activities are often done out of compulsion to comply with the state's rules. True societal care comes from reliable and selfless individuals. Mahatma Gandhi emphasized, "Service can have no meaning unless one takes pleasure in it. When done for show or fear of public opinion, it stuns the man and crushes his spirits. Service which is rendered without joy helps neither the servant nor the served"

Selfless service

Swami Vivekananda, the great Indian Philosopher once said,

"If you want to meet God, serve man." Selfless service is not only a job or task to be performed; but an act of kindness which connects you with society. It opens your heart to radiate your love for others.

Engaging in selfless service is one of the most remarkable acts a human being can undertake. The most accurate form of selfless service involves giving without any expectation of receiving in return. This embodies the essence of genuine altruism, where our actions are motivated solely by the desire to assist others.

In this approach it is important to refrain from publicizing our deeds for the purpose of gaining admiration, praise, power or recognition. Instead shift the focus to sincere service from the depth of your heart and soul, driven by the genuine intention to support others.

Adopt kindness, spread love and help others and keep raising the bar. This giving spirit is a powerful gift that brings love and healing wherever we go. As a giver we not only comfort our own hearts but also foster personal growth, while recipients experience comfort, and understanding in our shared humanity. It connects us all.

Philosophy of selfless giving

Altruism and Altruistic behavior:

In the field of Ethology (the study of behavior), extensive research has explored altruism. Altruism is the behavioral commitment to enhance someone else's wellbeing, even at personal risk or cost. It is the selfless concern for others driven by a genuine desire to help rather than a sense of duty, loyalty or religious obligation.

Interestingly, humans and other creatures on earth also reflect altruistic behavior in their society.

Have you ever witnessed a group of monkeys moving together? You'll likely notice a prominent monkey, weather male or a female, leading the group. This individual provides direction and signals the group in case of any perceived danger.

The group exhibits highly evolved behavior, especially in the response to threat, as they unite and flee together. Vervet monkeys in particular reflect altruistic behavior. When one of them spots a predator, they emit a warning call diverting the predator's attention to themselves, and risking their own life for the safety and survival of the group. It's a remarkable display of selfless behavior.

Similarly, studies on honey bees show that they also reflect altruistic behavior within their colony. Not all the female' bees reproduce; only the queen bee does. The female worker bees increase their colony's overall fitness by caring for sisters. When they perceive any danger to the hive, eggs and babies of the territory, they use their stings even to the point of sacrificing their lives. In the process, at a certain stage the entire stinking apparatus is pulled from the bee's abdomen leading to its death. This extreme example illustrates the remarkable extend of altruistic behavior in honey bees.

Vampire Bats are another example of altruistic behavior animals. Studies showed that Bats feed on blood and will die in 70 hours of not eating. They survive by food sharing. They feed each other by regurgitating blood. This means they bring swallowed food up again to the mouth from their stomachs and share it with fellow bats. It's like they are un swallowing their food to help others in the colony. This cooperative act helps them all survive.

Later W.D. Hamilton also proved that nature supports this behavior in reproducing them and protecting their colonies.

There are so many examples of altruistic behavior in creatures and animals teaching us selflessness.

We never lose when we give. Many times, in life, we may have had the chance to help someone in need, making a sacrifice. Only to find that it was either returned to us or circumstances changed, and we did not need to sacrifice. Yet, we were rewarded with the satisfaction of having sacrificed for others.

However, being selfish, breeds remorse and regret. We may feel sorry for not giving. There is no greater joy than of giving. All those who have given selflessly would have experienced that one never loses when one passes instead, they find many more blessings showered upon them, unasked for, and their heart is filled with godly love.

Giving in the center of our profession: - Once you are convinced that your success depends on enabling others to succeed, you become the real professional.

Leadership emerges by sacrificing, guiding and teaching people that you work with. One can be a good writer by providing the readers with valuable content, knowledge, and entertainment. Likewise, entrepreneurial success is achieved by fostering a positive and conducive atmosphere to the employees and meeting customer requirements.

This conscious, intentional approach to give, enables us to contribute to our community, pushing the boundaries of our comfort zone. We may initially experience a hint of discomfort ourselves.

Legends such as Mahatma Gandhi, Abraham Lincoln, Nelson Mandela, Martin Luther King Jr., Mother Teresa and many others have set benchmarks for all of us by prioritizing society over self. Their remarkable deeds illuminate the path towards a more compassionate and altruistic existence.

In my experience with the social organization I'm part of, I've witnessed individuals achieving success while working internationally for humanity with great zeal. Those who dedicate themselves to the society, often find fulfillment in all aspects of life.

During the challenging times of the Covid Pandemic, many of us stayed safe by isolating in our homes, there were also heroes who selflessly prioritized other's well-being over themselves.

Some took responsibility for burying/burning the dead bodies, while others dedicated themselves to provide essential food and medicine to those in need. Some worked tirelessly to ensure safe home returns to students. Despite certain hospitals overcharging for the COVID treatment, there were selfless doctors and nurses who sacrificed their lives while treating patients. Additionally, there were numerous scientists who devoted months and years of their life for developing Vaccine for the disease.

Imagine the deep satisfaction and contentment these individuals felt, finding motivation from their own deeds. Acts of humanity not only ignite courage and boldness but also touch the core of our emotions.

Now as we wrap up, let the weight of these heartfelt questions sink in carrying the powerful essence of our shared humanity.

1) When did you extend a helping hand?

2) When was the time you were truly selfless?

3) When was the time you really lived your life and took the problem head on?

DO IT YOURSELF

1. Recollect the joy you felt when you sacrificed or donated something to needy last time.

2. Explore how you can incorporate the selfless giving formula into your job or profession you are in.

3. Observe the people in your society who are actively making others happy

4. Plan to donate your time, money or skill for your own joy and fulfillment.

5. What do you understand by service above self?